to
Shakespeare's

Antony and Cleopatra

by
Adrian Poole

Contents

Introduction   4

A summary of the plot   10

What is *Antony and Cleopatra* about?   14

Who is Cleopatra?   19

How does Cleopatra beguile Antony?   26

Why does Cleopatra call Antony
"Herculean"?   30

What does Antony mean to Caesar?   37

Why does Caesar sacrifice his sister?   43

What does Caesar feel for his sister?   45

Why does Caesar get so angry with his
sister?   50

How is Cleopatra's theatre different from
Caesar's?   52

Why does Shakespeare make so much of
Enobarbus?   59

How do you earn "a place in the story"?   63

What's special about the play's language?   78

What happens to Antony after Actium?   89

Is Cleopatra's death too beautiful?   94

Does it still make sense to think of the
play as a tragedy?   102

NOTES

The world of Antony and Cleopatra   8

Shakespeare and Rome   16

Divinities and heroes   20

Cleopatra and boys   22

Sexual allusions in Antony and Cleopatra   24

Dido and Aeneas   34

Religion and politics   40

Critics on Antony and Cleopatra   46

Cleopatra on stage   54

Six quotes to remember   61

Ten facts about Antony and Cleopatra   64

Antony's warrior   75

Three 20th-century views of Antony and Cleopatra   79

The lure of Egypt   86

What Shakespeare did with North's Plutarch   98

The play in performance   106

A short chronology   111

Bibliography   113

Introduction

Shakespeare's plays have not enjoyed uniform popularity over the past 400 years – the Victorians had much more time than we do for *Henry VIII* and no time at all for *Troilus and Cressida* – and *Antony and Cleopatra* is an interesting case in point. There is no record of it being performed in Shakespeare's lifetime. This does not mean that it wasn't, but if it had been a big hit we would surely have known it. From the Restoration onwards John Dryden's highly sanitised version held the stage, or as time went on, shared it with Shakespeare's. From Samuel Phelps's landmark production at Sadler's Wells in 1849 onwards Shakespeare's play gained more currency, mainly for comparatively shallow reasons to do with the opportunity for spectacle provided by the play's material and one of the title-characters.

Outside the theatre, in the hands of critics, readers and other artists, it was of course mainly Cleopatra and Egypt that caught the attention. Victorian writers, both male and female, eagerly debated the merits, virtues and lessons to be learned from the array of Shakespeare's women, from Rosalind, Portia, Imogen, Ophelia, Cordelia, and Lady Macbeth. The last named was linked by John Ruskin in an unholy trinity with Regan and Goneril, "frightful exceptions to the ordinary laws of life". Cleopatra was one of three notable women about whom he had nothing to say (the others were Gertrude and Cressida); she left him speechless. When Dickens wants to mock an ageing woman trying to exert her failing charms on Mr Dombey, it is the serpent of old Nile to whom he compares her. Other writers, including women writers, could be more appreciative. Anna Jameson admired Cleopatra's contradictions, "fused into one brilliant impersonation of classical elegance, Oriental voluptuousness, and gipsy sorcery". George Eliot chose as a chapter epigraph bearing on the chastened female protagonist of *Daniel Deronda*, Gwendolen Harleth, Cleopatra's words, "My desolation does begin to make a better life". When John Keats wanted to describe the attraction he felt for a handsome young woman he called her a "Charmian", carefully distinguishing her from a "Cleopatra". When Henry James sought to suggest the charm cast over an impressionable but repressed American by a glamorous Parisian countess, it was Cleopatra's "infinite variety" to which he had recourse.

There are two obvious reasons why the play has enjoyed a great leap in popularity and interest since the early decades of the 20th century. One is to do with changing attitudes to gender and sexuality, already at work in the later 19th century, relaxing some (though certainly not all) of the taboos impeding the liberation of women from the confinements and distinctions in force at least since the Restoration. The other is to do with changing conceptions of theatre. The advent of cinema liberated theatre from the responsibility of providing mass popular and spectacular entertainment, and permitted the return to lighter, swifter and more flexible forms of staging. One can scarcely think of a Shakespeare play that benefits more from such a liberation in so far as it is required to wield a great bulk (of material, events, characters) at varying degrees of speed, some of them very swift.

But there are other less obvious reasons. One involves the opposition between love and romance on the one hand and politics and war on the other – the play's complex re-working of some age-old myths about Venus and Mars. The play received a new lease of life early in the 19th century, the so-called "Romantic" period, when it became possible to view it as more than the moral fable it had seemed, from the Restoration onwards, about the catastrophic effects of passion, and the incompatibility of Pleasure and Virtue – the Roman reading. Linda Charnes puts it like this:

> The increasing popularity of the play has been inseparable from a critical revisionism that has transformed it from what it was in Shakespeare's time – a notorious story about politics on every level – to what it is now: a "legendary" love story about Great Individuals in Love. (*Notorious*

Identity: Materializing the Subject in Shakespeare, Harvard University Press, 1993)

This story begins with the Romantics and still to some extent holds sway today. But it has also become contested – not least by critics like Charnes – by interpretations that see the politics and the love affair as inextricably combined. As our own media daily insist, at least in the anglophone world, the love-affairs of the top dogs *are* matters of public interest. The fate of all those men and women sacrificed "to solder up the rift" between Antony and Caesar does hang on what happens, or fails to happen, behind the scenes.

Charlton Heston and Hildegarde Neil during the filming of the 1972 film of Antony and Cleopatra. *Heston directed the film as well as playing Antony.*

THE WORLD OF
ANTONY AND CLEOPATRA

82-30BC Mark Antony (Marcus Antonius)

69-30BC Cleopatra VII

63 BC – AD 14
Octavius Caesar (born Gaius Octavius; on adoption by Julius Caesar, he took the name Gaius Julius Caesar Octavianus; on becoming the first Emperor, known as Augustus)

BC

51 Cleopatra succeeds her father Ptolemy XII as joint ruler of Egypt, with her younger brother Ptolemy XIII, to whom she is nominally married

48 Julius Caesar defeats Pompey the Great at the Battle of Pharsalus; Pompey is murdered. Cleopatra ousted in civil war with her brother but reinstated by Caesar and becomes effectively sole ruler of Egypt

47 Cleopatra gives birth to a son, Caesarion, supposedly fathered by Caesar

47-44 Julius Caesar dictator

46-44 Cleopatra in Rome

44 Julius Caesar is murdered

43 The triumvirate of Mark Antony, Lepidus and Octavius Caesar is appointed for five years

42 Mark Antony and Octavius Caesar defeat the republicans Brutus and Cassius at the battle of Philippi; Julius Caesar deified

41 Antony and Cleopatra meet on the river Cydnus at Tarsus in Cilicia

41-40	Antony in Alexandria; Cleopatra gives birth to twins
40	Death of Antony's wife, Fulvia. Hostilities between Antony and Octavius Caesar settled by the Treaty of Brundisium; Antony marries the latter's widowed half-sister, Octavia
39	Meeting of Sextus Pompeius and the Triumvirs at Misenum
37	Triumvirate renewed for a further five years; Antony leaves Rome and resumes his relationship with Cleopatra
36	Antony's unsuccessful campaign in Parthia. Lepidus ousted from the triumvirate.
34	Antony subdues Armenia and returns to Cleopatra. In the Donations of Alexandria, lands and titles are distributed to Cleopatra and her children
33	Preparations for war between Antony and Octavius Caesar
32	Antony divorces Octavia; Rome declares war on Cleopatra
31	Octavius Caesar defeats Antony and Cleopatra at the sea-battle of Actium
30	Battle of Alexandria; Mark Antony and Cleopatra commit suicide
27	Octavius Caesar receives the title of Augustus, together with 'Imperator' (literally, 'general') and 'Princeps' (literally, 'first citizen').
	AD
14	Augustus, the first Roman 'Emperor', dies

A summary of the plot

Before the play

In *Julius Caesar* Shakespeare dramatised the key events in Roman history that precede this play: the murder of Julius Caesar by a group of conspirators led by Brutus and Cassius, and their defeat at the battle of Philippi by the joint forces of the "triumvirate", the coalition of Mark Antony, Lepidus and Caesar's great-nephew and adopted heir, Octavius. The stage is poised for a battle of power between the two dominant triumvirs, Antony and the young Octavius Caesar.

Act I

The play opens in Egypt, where Queen Cleopatra has been royally entertaining the great Roman general, Mark Antony, with all the sensual delights dreamed of by a war-weary veteran. We will in due course learn of previous Roman generals who have fallen under her charms – Julius Caesar and "great Pompey". Messengers arrive from Rome with news that Antony cannot afford to ignore: the troubles stirred up by his wife, Fulvia, and then her death, but also the threat posed by a new rising star, Sextus Pompeius, another son of Pompey the Great, vanquished rival of Julius Caesar. A first glimpse of Octavius Caesar – known in this play simply as "Caesar" – confirms the abhorrence but also the fascination that Antony's dalliance with

Cleopatra excites back in Rome. Antony prepares
to leave Egypt. Cleopatra and her entourage
will entertain themselves as best they can in his
absence.

Act II

At a summit-meeting in Rome, Antony and Caesar
give vent to their mutual grievances. In a bid to
reconcile the two men, one of Caesar's henchmen
proposes a political marriage between Antony
and Caesar's half-sister, Octavia, which Antony
accepts. Preparations are made to deal with young
Pompey. Antony's right-hand man, Enobarbus,
regales his open-mouthed comrades with tales
of Egypt, above all the meeting of Antony and
Cleopatra on the river Cydnus. Provoked by his
Soothsayer, Antony is already being drawn back to
Cleopatra: "I'th'East my pleasure lies". Meanwhile
news of his marriage to Octavia reaches Cleopatra,
who takes out her fury on the messenger. In
another tense political encounter at Mount
Misena the triumvirs and Pompey negotiate a deal,
and celebrate aboard the latter's galley. One of the
pirates who have joined up with Pompey offers
to murder the triumvirs but Pompey demurs.
Everyone gets drunk, even Caesar.

Act III

In a brief but incisive scene the action is
transported to Syria where Antony's lieutenant,

Ventidius, has brought off a stunning victory over Rome's long-standing enemies, the Parthians, but prudently declines to promote himself further. Attention switches to the union of Antony and Octavia, which rapidly disintegrates under the mutual recriminations of her husband and brother. She returns to Rome, to be greeted by news of the latest scandal in Egypt. Antony and Cleopatra have put on a huge public demonstration of their claims, and their children's, to sovereignty over a great swathe of "the East". The stage is set for war. A dizzying series of short scenes leads up to the climactic battle of Actium, where Antony, urged on by Cleopatra, makes the catastrophic choice to fight by sea. Cleopatra takes flight and Antony follows her, leaving Caesar the undisputed victor. The humiliated Antony rages at Cleopatra but they make up, only for Antony's fury to erupt again when he thinks she is preparing to negotiate with Caesar through another hapless messenger, Thidias. Again the lovers make up, and Antony prepares for one more "gaudy night". But Enobarbus's loyalty has been shaken and he prepares to abandon his master.

Act IV
In an act that consists of no less than 16 short scenes (in modern editions), the tug of war between Caesar and Antony continues. The play is now firmly set in Egypt, in and around Cleopatra's

capital, Alexandria. In a mysterious night-time scene Antony's soldiers hear strange music which they take to mean that the god Hercules is now leaving their master. The same night Enobarbus deserts to Caesar. Antony generously sends the man's treasure after him, prompting the soldier who brings it to comment: "Your Emperor / Continues still a Jove". Enobarbus's heart is breaking. Antony wins a first encounter with Caesar's forces by land, but a second by sea ends in hopeless capitulation. Between the two battles Enobarbus dies in misery and shame. The final defeat sends Antony into yet another rage at what he believes to be Cleopatra's betrayal. In terror she takes refuge in her Monument and sends news of her suicide. Believing her to be dead, Antony tries also to kill himself but fails, and has to be hauled up to the Monument to be reunited with her. He dies in her arms, and she seems ready to join him in death, "after the high Roman fashion".

Act V

By contrast with the frenetic toing and froing of the previous two Acts, the final one consists of only two scenes. In the first Caesar receives news of Antony's death, and plans how to capture Cleopatra alive. The second is set in Cleopatra's Monument where she receives a series of visitors, including two of Caesar's emissaries, with one of whom she shares her dream of an Emperor

Antony: "His legs bestrid the ocean..." Dolabella is charmed into telling her the truth about his master's intentions to lead her back to Rome in triumph – and humiliation. She receives Caesar himself, and resolves to thwart his plans and rejoin her beloved Antony. In a scene of astonishingly precarious comedy, a rural fellow brings her the means of release, a basket of figs concealing some snakes ("aspics"). Clothed in her most regal attire, and in her most magnificent manner, Cleopatra dies, along with her two loyal handmaidens, Iras and Charmian. Caesar arrives too late to do more than look down on the "lass unparalleled", and make arrangements for the famous pair to be buried together with "great solemnity".

What is *Antony and Cleopatra* about?

Over the last 100 years or so *Antony and Cleopatra* has attracted increasing admiration from writers, readers, critics and audiences. The poet W. H. Auden declared: "If we had to burn all of Shakespeare's plays but one – luckily we don't – I'd choose *Antony and Cleopatra.*" T. S. Eliot also greatly admired it. In *The Waste Land* he re-works its single most famous speech, the description of Cleopatra's spectacular first meeting with Antony on the river Cydnus: "The barge she sat in, like a

Laurence Olivier and Vivien Leigh as Antony and Cleopatra in a 1951 film adaptation

burnished throne, / Burned on the water..." We might reflect that it takes a very special kind of fire to burn on *water*. For Virginia Woolf, too, the play typified the genius of Shakespeare. In *A Room of One's Own* she wrote: "the mind of an artist, in order to achieve the prodigious effort of freeing whole and entire the work that is in him, must be incandescent like Shakespeare's mind, I conjectured, looking at the book which lay open at *Antony and Cleopatra.*"

"Incandescent" is a fine word, suggestive of fire and light and brilliance, of passionate rage and scintillating wit. All these qualities are to be

SHAKESPEARE AND ROME

Antony and Cleopatra is one of several plays Shakespeare wrote about Rome, and Roman history. Probably written in 1606–7, it can be read in close conjunction with *Coriolanus* (1607–8), the two last tragedies that he composed. (The first text of the play we have comes from the First Folio (1623); quotations in this book are taken from Michael Neill's edition for Oxford World's Classics (1994).) It can also be read alongside *Julius Caesar* (1599), which inaugurated the period in which tragedy dominated Shakespeare's writing (and his company took possession of the Globe theatre on the south bank of the Thames).

These two plays concentrate on the most dramatic phase of Roman history, the protracted

found in Cleopatra – one of Shakespeare's most extraordinary creations – the queen who will boast as she nears her end that she's finished with the baser elements of earth and water: "I am fire and air."

The play is about the most famous love affair in the ancient world. It is about sex and death. But it is also about power and politics, about how history gets made. This is what makes it so extraordinary, that everything and everyone is interconnected, the sex and the politics, what happens in bed, on the battlefield and in the council-chamber, what brings together the superstar, the nobody

turmoil in which the Republic collapsed and gave slow, painful birth to the Empire. So that *Antony and Cleopatra* can be understood and performed as a sequel to *Julius Caesar*. It continues the story left poised at the end of the earlier play, when the new triumvirate of Antony, Octavius Caesar and Lepidus have defeated at Philippi the leaders of the conspiracy to murder Julius Caesar – Brutus and Cassius. In the later play Antony will remember all too vividly the battle of Philippi, when his younger partner, so he claims, "kept his sword like a dancer". In *Coriolanus* Shakespeare reverted to a much earlier moment in Roman history, the birth of the Republic (510 BC) of which the other two plays showed the demise. In the modern theatre this means you can present the three plays in a sequence corresponding to the historical realities (as with the two sequences of Shakespeare's English history plays), beginning with *Coriolanus* and ending with *Antony and Cleopatra* ∎

and the wannabe. In no play of Shakespeare's do more things happen across a wider geographical space to a larger number of people. It is about two individuals larger than life, but it is also about all the other lives they touch and are touched by.

Antony and Cleopatra were real people, not the matter of fiction or myth or pre-history, like Dido and Aeneas or Troilus and Cressida. These three stories were in Shakespeare's time extremely well known; everyone knew how they ended – badly. There is of course another Shakespeare play about love, which has now become the most famous of them all. But to its first audiences *Romeo and Juliet* would have appeared modern, something fashionable from Italy, not dignified with the aura of legend nor laden with its inevitability.

Could the story have turned out differently? Was it all fated, determined, meant to be? These are questions that tragedy always asks, but never more sharply than in *Antony and Cleopatra,* where "the story" does not just concern the two title-characters but the whole known world they inhabited – *and* the subsequent course of Western history. The play stages a critical moment in time when Rome established its dominance over Europe and the Mediterranean, just before the birth of Christ. "The time of universal peace is near," proclaims the man who will become the Emperor Augustus. It is one of many dreams, visions and prophecies uttered in the course of the play. What if the battle of Actium had gone the other way, and Cleopatra's dream of an Emperor Antony had come true? What if Alexandria had become the centre of the Western world instead of Rome? What if the West had been easternised? For this play is also about "what if".

Who is Cleopatra?

She is Queen of the East, sovereign of everything that's opposed to Rome, its values, its virtues, its beliefs. No wonder she inspires fear and desire in every self-respecting Roman – or more exactly, every Roman male. All good Roman men are fascinated, intrigued and obsessed by her. As for the man she has taken as her lover, he excites in his fellow-Romans envy, admiration, and disgust. They can't always tell which is which.

Listen to the opening speech of the play by one Roman to another, who has just arrived in Egypt. Look what Cleopatra has done to our man, he complains, to the heroic and legendary Antony. She has reduced him to "dotage", a state of abject, unmanly servitude. This is the voice of the (Ro)man-in-the-street, the purveyor of scandal and gossip and cliché, of which we shall hear a great deal. Having seen for himself, the newcomer (Demetrius) will confirm that this is exactly what "the common liar" is saying back in Rome. They are foreigners here in Egypt, the two of them,

DIVINITIES AND HEROES

Aeneas Trojan hero, lover of Dido, queen of Carthage, whom he abandoned for his mission to found Rome

Ajax also referred to as Telamon, Greek hero renowned for his defensive powers, who went mad and killed himself after losing the contest for Achilles's armour

Dido queen of Carthage and lover of Aeneas, who slew herself when he left her

Gorgon mythological snake-haired monster, also known as Medusa, who turned anyone who looked on her to stone

Hector heroic warrior of Troy

Hercules mythological figure of strength, endurance and appetite, also known as Alcides; killed by a poisoned robe ("the shirt of Nessus"), sent by his wife, Deianira, in the mistaken belief that it would magically win back his love

Isis Egyptian moon, earth and fertility goddess*

Jove supreme deity, father of the gods, also known as Jupiter

Juno queen of the gods, consort of Jupiter

Lichas the herald who delivered the poisoned robe to Hercules, and was hurled to his death

Mars god of war

Mercury god of messengers

Narcissus mythological figure of youthful male beauty, who fell in love with his own reflection

Neptune god of the sea

Nereides sea-nymphs, daughters of the sea-god Nereus

Nessus the Centaur, half-man, half-horse, who avenged his own death at Hercules's hands by giving the lethal potion to his killer's wife, Deianira

Phoebus god of the sun

Venus goddess of love

*The only non-Roman deity

tourists in a sense, giving vent to "prejudice" in the strict sense of the word – a judgment reached in advance. They know what they are going to see. Cleopatra fulfils all the worst expectations of the prurient moralist: she is a "gypsy", a "strumpet", a "whore", all the bad words you can think of to express male fear for a desirable woman. She's a witch who has cast a spell over our hero and turned him into her sex slave. We could activate the kind of sexual pun of which the play itself is full, and say that the play opens with Cleopatra "on top".

"Behold and see". This man is the announcer, the theatrical compère. He introduces "the show", not just to his friend but also to us. His cartoon-

CLEOPATRA AND BOYS

We should never entirely forget that in Shakespeare's theatre the role of Cleopatra was played by a boy. Indeed there's a case for thinking that a boy might be more effective in freeing the audience's imagination, rather than confusing them with their reactions to a real female figure in front of them. It would have to be a boy with an exceptional voice, who can distinguish himself from the other boy he imagines travestying his Cleopatra in Rome. Indeed whoever plays the role, he or she has to draw on vocal resources out of the ordinary, a great variety of tone, timbre, volume and quality ∎

captions provide a frame, a virtual arch, through which the title-characters make their entrance. It's grand and theatrical, and as soon as they open their mouths, we wonder how far they are putting on a performance, for the audience on stage as well as for us. They are truly a great double act.

CLEOPATRA
If it be love indeed, tell me how much.
ANTONY
There's beggary in the love that can be
reckoned.
CLEOPATRA
I'll set a bourn how far to be beloved.
ANTONY
Then must thou needs find out new heavens,
new earth. (1.i)

We can tell from this quick-witted banter how well-matched they are, what good sparring partners. If only all lovers could play like this. But these two are old hands. This is not for them "the first time", as it is for Romeo and Juliet and all the girls and boys of Shakespearean comedy, who find each other through such swift verbal exchange, through testing and teasing and trumping each other. It is sexy for sure to hear the two of them sparring like this, and yet it's almost too smooth a routine. It inspires all kinds of questions. Have they rehearsed it? Is it as pre-meditated as that

Roman observer's little speech was pre-judiced? Will we ever get to see them alone, without an audience on stage? Are they getting a bit old for this? How can we judge "if it be love *indeed*" – for her, for him, for the two of them? Cleopatra's question will resonate through the whole play – through all the tantrums and tears, the rages and curses and break-ups, the re-unions, the vows, the visions.

In 1813 Lord Byron went to see a version of the

SEXUAL ALLUSIONS IN *ANTONY AND CLEOPATRA*

Words and phrases with sexual connotations are common in this play, some blatant, others more suggestive. Most important of all is the pun, very common in Shakespeare's time, on "die" and "death", meaning "orgasm". When Charmian says "let him marry a woman that cannot go", she means "cannot copulate, have sex"; to "tumble" has a clear sexual reference, when Caesar thinks of what Antony's up to in Alexandria. If Cleopatra is "salt" (that is, "lecherous"), then Antony is "ne'er lust-wearied" (that is, as we might say, he "cannot get enough of it"). Images of food and eating, such as "fragment" and "morsel", are often associated with sex; so too are the actions of "ploughing" and "riding". Words associated with male and female sexual organs include "sword", "pole", "snake", "worm", and "fig", "case", "lap", "garland". See Gordon Williams, *A Glossary of Shakespeare's Sexual Language*, Athlone Press, 1997 ∎

play he describes as "a salad of Shakespeare and Dryden". (Some 60 years after Shakespeare's death, John Dryden re-worked the story into *All for Love, or The World Well Lost*, an infinitely tidier, shallower and more simply moralistic affair.) Cleopatra struck Byron as "the epitome of her sex – fond, lively, sad, tender, teasing, humble, haughty, beautiful, the devil! – coquettish to the last, as well with the 'asp' as with Antony... And the questions about Octavia – it is woman all over." It sounds as though he enjoyed himself. But one of the things Byron relishes is exactly the confidence in his own generalisation: "the epitome of her sex", "woman all over". He sounds like the men in the play, the Romans who try to explain what makes her unique – her endless capacity to surprise them.

None of them can be sure what Cleopatra will say or do next. They cannot find the means to contain her, even in death. Much of the play shows them trying to do exactly that, to find ways of putting her into words that will neutralise her capacity to catch them off guard, to outwit, outfox and outleap them. As for readers and audiences, reviewers and critics, they are lured into repeating the predicament of the characters within the play who want to put her in her place, or find a place to put her in. Some of them pass judgment; others confess their admiration; a few even half fall in love. All of them are somehow in thrall to her, especially Antony.

How does Cleopatra beguile Antony?

No sooner have the lovers completed their opening rally with the fantasy of finding "new heaven, new earth" than their game is interrupted. They were just getting going. The first of the play's many messengers bursts on stage, ironically echoing the very word Antony has airily used about heaven and earth, this time from a world that is all too real: "news... from Rome". When you are on vacation, news from home is the last thing you want. Antony is off-duty, on leave, taking a break. Rome is home, work, duty, restraint, responsibility; Egypt is abroad, holiday, freedom, excess. In a few scenes we shall meet his great "competitor", Octavius Caesar – he never takes a holiday – reporting with supreme distaste "the news" from Alexandria, about all the fun-and-games that Antony has been getting up to.

But in the meantime, in this opening scene, we watch the beginnings of a struggle between Rome and Egypt that will tear apart the lovers and their world. If the messenger from Rome interrupts the game, then Cleopatra interrupts *him* so he does not get to deliver his news. She guesses that it will all be about Antony's wife, Fulvia, and his emulous colleague, young Caesar. Brilliantly, she pretends to urge Antony to listen to the "messengers"(there seems to be more than one), and "ambassadors"

– how many are there queuing up, we wonder? But she does it with such extravagance that she makes it into a kind of test, for herself no less than for him. "I know Fulvia and Caesar and Rome are more important to you than I am. Go ahead, desert and betray me!" This is another way of asking "how much do you love me?" But it's also, "can I get you to do just what I want?" What a crafty trickster she is, and how easily Antony falls for it, hook line and sinker, just as he falls for the trick with the salted fish we shall hear about later. There's never any shortage of jests and japes, of charades and masquerades here in Egypt. "Let Rome in Tiber melt," Antony famously declares. To that listening pair of Romans who started the scene off, this must sound near-blasphemy.

How does it sound to us? Magnificent, for one thing. "The nobleness of life / Is to do thus," he says, embracing Cleopatra in public. Crazy too, for we must know at some level that the holiday can't last for ever. And yet, if you *were* to give everything up for passion, wouldn't someone like Cleopatra be just the partner to choose – "Whom everything becomes – to chide, to laugh, / To weep – ..."? Wouldn't this be the person to play with, as the mood took you both, to wander through the streets by night, a couple in the crowd, at once alone and surrounded by others, a heaven on earth within easy reach? No, let's do without the news, for the time being.

We all know what it means to "lose track of time", when we're asleep, or just dreamy, or wholly absorbed in something that takes us out of ourselves and the sense of time passing. Egypt is the name for such a state of being. "Here is my space," Antony defiantly proclaims. There are no clocks here, any more than there are in the Forest of Arden, or anywhere else to which people escape from the city, where the laws get made, the money is earned, the crowns are conferred and punishments exacted.

And yet the play's second scene does not quite confirm this vision of Egypt as a land of absolute ease and contentment. In a way that's typical of Shakespeare we now get to see behind the scenes for a moment. Here's Cleopatra's entourage, her ladies-in-waiting Charmian and Iras, her servants Alexas and Mardian, the eunuch – and Antony's right-hand-man Enobarbus, who has made himself at home with them. They are eating and drinking and fooling around, speaking in prose.

But the foolery has a slight edge to it. It revolves around a soothsayer, from whom they are trying to extricate news – of the future. He speaks in verse, which marks him apart. As in that opening scene, where the Egyptian world of relaxed comic banter was shot through with Roman anxieties, so here the maids' frivolity is chilled by the soothsayer's sober, enigmatic pronouncements. They do not know what he means, and neither perhaps does he.

But he serves to remind them that there *is* a future ahead. The fun will not last forever. He is a special kind of messenger, touched with the supernatural, a remnant of other-worldly powers that were much more blatant in *Julius Caesar*, with its omens, its cosmic storm and its vengeful ghost. He will reappear at a crucial moment, to urge Antony back from Rome to Egypt.

But here and now in Egypt Antony is being forced in the other direction. The news from Rome will not be denied. His wife Fulvia and brother Lucius have made war on each other, then joined forces against Caesar. A former ally, Labienus, has gone over to Rome's old enemy, Parthia – like Scotland or France in the English history plays – and conquered a vast tract of the near East. A second messenger arrives and a third: there is more news. Fulvia is dead.

Et in Arcadia Ego runs the ancient epitaph on the tomb in the happy land, declaring either with the voice of the deceased that "I too have lived in Arcadia", or with the voice of Death itself that "Even in Arcadia I cannot be avoided". Antony has been living the good life in the happy land where time seems to stop. But it hasn't. Mortality has broken in. And there's yet another urgent reason to rush back to Rome: the new threat embodied by a rising star of the next generation, Sextus Pompeius. Time to break free of the strong Egyptian fetters, the spell cast by the beautiful witch, before he loses himself in – the word we heard in the play's very first line – "dotage".

Why does Cleopatra call Antony "Herculean"?

To say that Cleopatra is displeased by the news of his imminent departure would be an understatement. She is expert at tantrums. "Look, prithee, Charmian, / How this Herculean Roman does become / The carriage of his chafe," says Cleopatra, tauntingly. In other words: he looks the part when he gets angry like this, doesn't he? She means the part of Hercules, famous for his anger (or Senecan "furor") amongst other things. "Herculean" would have been an even more outlandish word for Shakespeare's first audience than it is to us. (They would have heard it stressed on the second syllable: "Hercúlean".)

There is more than a tinge of mockery to the twist she is giving to the noun "Hercules". Cleopatra is not jesting when she says that Antony is painted "one way like a Gorgon, the other way's a Mars". She's describing a visual puzzle or enigma, the whole point of which is its reversibility: look at him from one side he's a Mars, from the other he's a Gorgon. This is confusing to say the least.

Opposite: Richard Burton and Elizabeth Taylor in the 1963 film directed by Joseph L. Mankiewicz. At the time, Cleopatra *was the most expensive film ever made.*

The Gorgon is an archetype of murderous female power, to be slain by the heroic male – Perseus, to be precise, though Mars would be a fair substitute. What kind of monstrous creature *is* this man she's in love with? Is he as puzzling to her as she is to him? Is this one of the grounds for the passion between them, that they can't understand each other – and this is exciting?

"Hercules" represents a particular idea of manhood and masculinity. It is less powerful in the west now than it once was, though we still recognise it in certain kinds of sportsmen and movie stars and fantasy heroes, the he-men and hunks with rippling muscles. The motto of Shakespeare's most famous theatre showed Hercules carrying a Globe on his shoulders. In ancient myth Hercules was the epitome of strength, courage and endurance. He was one of humanity's two great philanthropists, the counterpart in the physical world of Prometheus in the mental. Between them they set us on the path towards culture, one clearing the world of wild beasts, the other teaching us the skills to make sense of and master it.

But there is more to Hercules than this, because there are so many legends about him, including stories about the mad rage in which he kills his own wife and children, and the rage of agony induced by the poisoned robe of Nessus, when he hurls the herald Lichas into the sea. There is also the "fame" of his humiliating enslavement to the oriental queen, Omphale, who forced him to wear women's clothes and do women's work. This story commended itself to the historical Caesar who had no qualms about applying it to Antony. The play itself alludes to it, in the story of Cleopatra dressing him in her clothes while she wears his sword "Philippan". Closely akin to this is the story of Mars's undoing by Venus, the god of war unmanned by sexual desire, referred to by the eunuch Mardian (appropriately enough, given the sound of his name: this is what happens to "Mars" when he gets "marred"). And finally there is the story, so popular in the Renaissance, of the Choice of Hercules, between Virtue and Pleasure, embodied in two beautiful women, according to which he chose, like a good boy, the former.

Antony was supposedly descended from Hercules, or Alcides (another name for him), and Plutarch says that he looked like him. * Quite how like and unlike Antony is to these great male

* Shakespeare made great use of Plutarch, in the Elizabethan translation by Sir Thomas North, for all his Roman plays. But the story of Antony and Cleopatra was very well-known in the 16th century. It had been the subject of various plays before Shakespeare's, including Giraldi Cinthio's *Cleopatra* (1542) and Robert Garnier's *Marc Antoine* (1578). Shakespeare is unlikely to have known any of these directly, but Garnier's may have reached him via the Countess of Pembroke's translation in the 1590s. He certainly seems to have known the play by her protégé, Samuel Daniel, *The Tragedy of Cleopatra,* first published in 1599, and again (revised) in 1607.

archetypes – Mars, Hercules – is one of the play's big teasing questions. One answer would be that lots of people in the play (including Antony himself) *would like him to be like them*, or even to believe that he *is* them – then register various degrees of disappointment that he isn't. At the very start those Roman commentators set the tone in talking about his "dotage" and his captain's heart reneging "all temper".

Later there are two key moments. One is the eery night-scene in Alexandria, when the soldiers hear the music, and interpret this to mean that it is "the god Hercules, whom Antony lov'd/ Now

DIDO AND AENEAS

Another set of misfitting parallels is provided by the story of Dido and Aeneas. There is certainly an analogy to be drawn between the two love-affairs: both Dido and Cleopatra were great North African queens whose destiny gets entangled with Rome. Antony seems to remember this. When

he hears the (false) news of Cleopatra's suicide, he promises to follow her:

> *Eros! – I come, my queen.*
> *– Eros! – Stay for me.*
> *Where souls do couch*
> *on flowers we'll hand in*
> *hand,*
> *And with our sprightly*
> *port make the ghosts*
> *gaze.*
> *Dido and her Aeneas*
> *shall want troops,*
> *And all the haunt be ours.*
> *(IV.xiv)*

But, leaving aside the ungainliness of that phrase

leaves him". Doesn't it seem odd that they should say this, rather than, as we might have expected, "the god Hercules, who lov'd Antony"? It is certainly unexpected that it should be Hercules and not the god Bacchus (Roman equivalent of the Greek Dionysus), as it had been in Shakespeare's source, Plutarch's *Lives of the Noble Grecians and Romans.* But the last indignity is incurred when Antony invokes the spirit of Hercules (or Alcides) in his death agony: "The shirt of Nessus is upon me – teach me / Alcides, thou mine ancestor, thy rage: / Let me lodge Lichas on the horns o'th'moon".

What good will that do? Who does Antony

"sprightly port", one wonders what version of the story Antony knows. Aeneas famously deserted the beloved Dido in favour of his duty to found Rome, choosing Virtue over Pleasure. And in Virgil at least, she never forgave him.

It is true that the historical Mark Antony could not yet have read Virgil's great rendition of the scene in the underworld, in which Dido with magnificent dignity turns her back on Aeneas in silence – "the most telling snub in all poetry," T. S.

Eliot called it. If he had read the *Aeneid* Antony would find himself constantly portrayed "as a negative measure of Virgil's hero", so John Gillies observes (*Shakespeare and the Geography of Difference*, Cambridge, 1994). The chances of Dido and Aeneas dancing together through the afterlife are slim to say the least, and the "sprightly port" with which Antony selects his comparison seems gruesomely ill-advised. Not for the first or last time, it leaves him sounding just a bit stupid ∎

suppose in his desperate plight to be Lichas (the hapless herald in the ancient myth)? "The witch shall die!" he exclaims. But if he's associating Cleopatra with Deianeira, who sent the poisoned robe that killed Hercules, then he is forgetting that she was innocent, poor woman, the victim of the Centaur, Nessus, and his malignant cunning. The parallels are all askew (see p.34).

Antony and Cleopatra may wish to be unique, "inimitable", but they can't manage without some reference to precedents, paradigms or ideals by which to be measured. The ancient world was full of such models, Graeco-Roman divinities such as Mars and Venus and Thetis, semi-divinities such as Hercules and Aeneas, the Egyptian goddess Isis. It was a world in which the boundaries between the human and the divine were indistinct, in a way less readily conceivable to a Christian world view. Shakespeare's King Richard II may believe that God's angels are on his side, and Hamlet's uncle Claudius may claim there's a divinity doth hedge a king, but Antony and Cleopatra are closer to believing in their own and each other's divinity. Closer, that is, to what would sound like blasphemy to Christian ears – save that these poor pagans couldn't be expected to have known any better.

What does Antony mean to Caesar?

When we first see Caesar he is complaining about Antony to the third man in the triumvirate set up to fill the power vacuum after Julius Caesar's murder. Lepidus is a hopeless nonentity, doomed to fail in his role as peacekeeper between the two alpha males. Caesar is Antony's polar opposite, coldly calculating, self-controlled, always at work.

It's a kind of opposition we have seen before in Shakespeare, between two types of men, one reckless, boisterous and magnanimous, the other prudent, reserved and ruthless. In *Henry IV Part One*, Hotspur and Hal partly answer to this oppositional scheme. From a distance at least, the extrovert seems to belong to the past, a yesterday's man who will no longer thrive in a modern world better suited to the businesslike type with an eye to the future. Closer up, a Prince Hal does begin to look more complicated. But Shakespeare was certainly reflecting on larger cultural shifts around him to which later ages can easily find parallels, as power passes from one generation to the next. The ageing man thinks of the newcomer as a mere "boy" and the younger man thinks of the other as an "old ruffian". This is how Antony and Caesar speak of each other, with classic mutual disrespect.

But there are interesting hints that Antony

plays a more complex role than this in young Caesar's imagination. We first hear Caesar bemoaning the antics of this increasingly unreliable colleague, wasting his time in Alexandria, cavorting with foreigners. But the terms in which he does so reveal a deeply puritanical streak reminiscent of Angelo in *Measure for Measure*. All this sex, drugs and rock'n'roll that Antony is indulging in can't possibly be good for him, thinks Caesar; it's bound to mean "Full surfeits and the dryness of his bones" – malaise and disease, the just punishment for debauchery. That might be all very well if he were doing this in his "vacancy" (that is, "vacation"), but when you're ruling the Roman Empire you have no such thing as "free time".

Then Shakespeare pulls one of his masterstrokes. In the narrative by Plutarch on which he relied for so much of this play, there is a passage describing an earlier phase in Antony's career, when the legend was born of his near superhuman, his "Herculean" strength and stamina – not a tale of triumph, but of suffering endured. At the battle of Modena, so the story goes, Antony was defeated and forced into the wilderness where he nearly starved to death. But he survived, drinking horses' urine and stagnant water, eating berries and tree-bark. Shakespeare follows this passage in Plutarch closely, but of course when you turn narrative into drama you have to put things into particular characters' mouths. The stroke of genius here is to give this story to Caesar, and make him deliver it, as if in a kind of trance, to the absent Antony:

> *On the Alps*
> *It is reported thou didst eat strange flesh,*
> *Which some did die to look on. (I.iv)*

It suggests that this young man once hero-worshipped Antony, and cannot forgive him for betraying the legend, or even quite believe that he has. It is a wonderful way of implying a whole "back-story" to the two men's relations.

Young Caesar is speaking here not just for himself but for a whole myth, the popular Roman view of Antony. Of course the young man's admiration may be tinged with envy or resentment at being provoked to such feelings. What is more, the woman who has now taken possession of Antony was the lover both of Caesar's (adoptive) father, the legendary Julius, and of young Pompey's. And for his part, Antony keeps expressing his disdain for young Caesar, the boy, the novice. How dare he. Marjorie Garber suggests the "Oedipal" aspect to this play, "full of submerged and smouldering love and resentment, expressed toward Antony, the father figure, the reminder and rebuker of sons". She has in mind young Pompey as well as young Caesar.

There is some reason for thinking in these terms. Antony does belong to an older generation. And yet the Oedipal model does not quite fit as it did in *Julius Caesar* where the title character was much more of a father figure, slain by the band of brothers, and betrayed above all by the man he has thought of as a son, Brutus. Antony too was then one of Julius Caesar's "sons", or seemed to be, and this should put him on the same level as Octavius, the grand-nephew, and, crucially, legal

RELIGION AND POLITICS

Shakespeare was well aware of the infidels in his world, especially of the Jews and Turks, adherents of the other most powerful monotheisms. And he was conscious of the agonising hostilities within a religion nominally unified under the name of Christianity. In his own country Catholics and Protestants had been torturing and killing each other for more than half a century, and the Puritans were gaining in power and ambition. These were urgent and potentially lethal differences of faith, for which some were prepared to risk their lives; many others were prepared to compromise and hedge their bets.

This is where Rome and the ancient world came in handy. It was so much less of a threat. Unlike the God of the Old Testament or of Islam, the divinities in which those pagans believed were a magnificent multitude, teetering on the brink of absurdity. Jupiter, Juno, Mars, Venus, Neptune, Mercury, Bacchus, Thetis – and Isis: nobody could possibly believe in them in

heir to the name of Caesar. This would make the relation between Antony and the young Caesar more that of siblings, older and younger brothers. In reality Antony was indeed old enough to be young Caesar's father – there were nearly 20 years between them – but Shakespeare chooses to blur the age-gap. There are strong shadowy passions at work here, in the triangular relations between Antony, Cleopatra and Caesar, but they are not clearly identifiable with the models of

the same sense that they were compelled to believe in one god. And yet those antique figures still made a kind of sense. Indeed the Renaissance gave a massive new currency to the old myths and legends such that they could run parallel to, or even athwart, the orthodoxies of Christian belief with its own tales of saints and martyrs.

The ancient stories provided a way of expressing passions, impulses, energies and desires towards which Christian doctrine seemed unmerciful and even uncomprehending. Nevertheless comparisons between ancient and

contemporary history could still be dangerous. If you chose to retell the story of Julius Caesar's murder, you were inviting questions about your own political beliefs. Shakespeare's contemporary, Fulke Greville, wrote a tragedy about Antony and Cleopatra, but he destroyed it for fear that the title characters might be identified with the reigning monarch, Queen Elizabeth, and her favourite, the Earl of Essex, declaring that "Antonie and Cleopatra, according to their irregular passions, in forsaking Empire to follow sensuality, were sacrificed to the fire. The executioner, the author himself." ▪

father and mother and son. There is indeed a trio of sons in the background, mothered all by Cleopatra, fathered by Julius Caesar and Antony, but the background is where they stay. Antony and Cleopatra evince (almost) no concern about them. And as for Caesar, so far as the play is concerned, he has no children, nor family life – apart from his beloved sister Octavia (and the briefest mention of a wife called Livia).

This is part of the point of this play's "world", the structure of its human relations, both political, familial and sexual. They do not enjoy the kind of clear distinctions between parents and children on which Shakespeare's earlier histories and tragedies depended, whether between fathers and sons (the *Henry IV* plays, *Julius Caesar*, *Hamlet*, *Macbeth*) or father and daughters (*King Lear*). If only Antony, the old ruffian, were more like a father, like Julius Caesar or old Hamlet or Claudius or Duncan. Instead, he behaves like a Falstaff. No wonder there's so much desperate emphasis on Antony's "sword" – the emblem of his martial and sexual prowess. What else is there left by which to recognize his manhood? No wonder the terms in which Cleopatra conceives her instant epitaph on his demise carry such mystery, or mystification: "The soldier's pole is fallen."

Why does Caesar sacrifice his sister?

The triumvirate that's supposed to rule Rome
and its Empire when the play starts is riven with
tensions. If this power-sharing arrangement is
to survive, and Rome to endure as a single entity,
then it's going to need some powerful motives,
agreements, concordats to hold it together. The
threat of young Pompey represents one such
good motive, but it's not hard to keep him at bay.
Everyone knows this won't be enough to hold the
"competitors" together. This is where Caesar's
sister Octavia comes in. If Pompey stands up
for the main soldier, then – to put it bawdily, as
Enobarbus might – Octavia has to lie down for the
main wife. In the tense encounter in Rome, when
Caesar and Antony come face to face for the first
time, it is Antony's arrangements with women
on which the negotiations dwell: the strong wife
Fulvia, difficult but dead; the Egyptian queen,
whore, what have you; and now, the proposed
solution, Caesar's half-sister, Octavia, the perfect
match for the widower Antony.

It is Caesar's henchman, Agrippa, who proposes
the move that will hold the two rivals (Lepidus
already doesn't count) "in perpetual amity". Caesar
has said they need a "hoop" to hold them "staunch,
from edge to edge / O'th'world" – as if the world

were a big barrel of beer. Later her brother will speak of Octavia as "cement", which he hopes will hold a fortress together rather than be turned into a battering ram. (Before she knows what news he brings, Cleopatra eagerly greets the messenger who will tell her of the marriage with the words: "Ram thou thy fruitful tidings in mine ears.") Poor Octavia. The contract is sealed by a formal handshake between Caesar and Antony, for all the world as if they were getting married to each other.

What does everyone expect from this frankly political marriage? The great Shakespearian critic A. C. Bradley rightly fixes on Caesar's motives in marrying his sister to Antony: "was he honest, or was he laying a trap and, in doing so, sacrificing his sister"? Does Caesar have any real hope that it will endure and do the trick it's supposed to, holding the barrel or fortress together? Or has he cynically worked out in advance that it's bound to fail, and that this will further discredit Antony in the eyes of the audience that matters most, the "slippery people"? The answer is that we can't know for sure. Harold Goddard suggests a contrast between the man who gives up an empire for a whore and the man who will whore his sister for an empire. A cynical view, to be sure, but one of the many the play asks us to contemplate. As for what Antony really thinks and feels about this marriage, who could possibly know when Antony himself doesn't seem to?

What does Caesar feel for his sister?

Caesar's sister Octavia does not have a large role in the play but it is of the greatest significance. There are hints of a tenderness and affection between them such as we do not see Caesar express for anyone else. And yet these hints are hard to perceive, or be sure of, and this suggests something more generally true of the expression of characters' inner lives in this play. We could say that they either tell us too much or not enough. Antony and Cleopatra are never short of words to express themselves, especially the latter, while Romans can give the impression they have nothing inside them to express. And in fact it's often said that the characters in Shakespeare's Roman plays generally lack the "inwardness" we find elsewhere, especially in tragedies such as *Hamlet* and *Macbeth*. They don't talk to themselves; we don't get to see them "in private", off-guard or off-stage; they don't confide in us.

Another way of putting it would be that these plays are just more sceptical about knowing what goes on inside people. When they're alone on stage, even Brutus and Cassius in *Julius Caesar* sound as though they are talking in public. The same is true of Coriolanus. We get just these glimpses and hints of the unspoken, perhaps the

Charlton Heston and Hildegarde Neil as Antony and Cleopatra in a 1972 film

CRITICS ON
ANTONY AND CLEOPATRA

❝ *That which is wanting to work up the pity to a greater height, was not afforded me by the story; for the crimes of love, which they both committed, were not occasioned by any necessity, or fatal ignorance, but were wholly voluntary; since our passions are, or ought to be, within our power.* **❞**

John Dryden, 1678

❝ *The continual hurry of the action, the variety of incidents, and the quick succession of one personage to another, call the mind forward, without intermission, from the first act to the last.* **❞**

Samuel Johnson, 1765

❝ *Shakespeare's genius has spread over the whole play a richness like the overflowing of the Nile.* **❞**

William Hazlitt, 1817

> 66 *She is not a Cleopatra, but she is at least a Charmian. She has a rich eastern look; she has fine eyes and fine manners. When she comes into a room she makes an impression the same as the Beauty of a Leopardess... I believe tho' she has faults – the same as Charmian and Cleopatra might have had. Yet she is a fine thing speaking in a worldly way... As a Man in the world I love the rich talk of a Charmian; as an eternal Being I love the thought of you. I should like her to ruin me, and I should like you to save me.* 99

John Keats, describing a young woman named Jane Cox to his sister-in-law Georgiana, 1818

> 66 *I simply adore this wild animal who wants Julius Caesar to sleep with her with his sword at his side, who assassinates poor Antony twenty times over, in ways most horrible, but who wishes not to outlive him and who in fact does not do so for long; this working girl with a crown who goes hopping in the streets of Alexandria, who has a 'salt fish' attached to Antony's line when he is fishing in the Nile, who in one hour changes her mind some twenty times; this daredevil who asks Mardian the eunuch about his amorous desires; this woman in the end at once ridiculous and cowardly who flees the field of the Battle of Actium without knowing why. What a character for a fantaisie musicale!* 99

Hector Berlioz, on Shakespeare's Cleopatra, 1859

unspeakable, when he addresses his wife as "My gracious silence", and holds his mother "by the hand, silent" (one of the few stage directions we can be sure is Shakespeare's own). How can we ever know what's not put into words, and how can we ever believe what is? The two most enigmatic characters in this play are Caesar and Cleopatra, for opposite reasons: the former so guarded, cautious, restrained, the other so uninhibited, extravagant, reckless. Both are perhaps always in some sense – performing.

Octavia is not particularly opaque. But she does participate in a peculiarly affecting and effective moment, when she says farewell to her brother, under the watchful eyes of her new husband, Antony. Her feelings are not hard to fathom, but what of the men's? Octavia wants to say something to her brother in private; she whispers in his ear. What does she say? We cannot hear. It is masked from us. In a world of such relentless and inventive eloquence, it is a moment of relief to find someone lost for words, and then to imagine instead of the hoops and cement and battering rams that surround her – a floating feather. The voice we hear at this moment is Antony's, and he invokes this image of exceptional sensitivity and beauty – as if he is intuiting something of Octavia's feelings for her brother, or her brother's feelings for her, or his own feelings for them both. Or even, magically and impossibly, feelings that belong to no one in particular and so, potentially, to everyone. It is an image that wonderfully captures a moment of stillness and poise at the centre of the play:

> *Her tongue will not obey her heart, nor can*
> *Her heart inform her tongue. The swan's-down*
> *feather*
> *That stands upon the swell at the full of tide,*
> *And neither way inclines. (III.ii)*

A moment to treasure. The next time we see Antony and Octavia together, the marriage is splitting apart and so is the world it was designed to "hoop" together. Octavia gives utterance to a vision of horror with almost prophetic force, as if her real name were Cassandra. At such a moment we look not only *into* Octavia but also *through* her:

> *Wars 'twixt you twain would be*
> *As if the world should cleave, and that slain men*
> *Should solder up the rift. (III.iv)*

A moment or two later, Enobarbus will match this with a gruff male equivalent. The two of them give utterance to the most "grown-up" vision of the consequences of war for the victims of the top dogs' shenanigans:

> *Then, world, thou hast a pair of chops [jaws], no*
> *more,*

And throw between them all the food thou hast,
They'll grind the one the other. (III.iv)

Octavia and Enobarbus: now that would make an interesting alliance.

Why does Caesar get so angry with his sister?

The scene commonly designated Act Three, Scene Six in modern editions stands at the play's very centre. Caesar and his advisors, Agrippa and Maecenas, have just received news of the spectacular show put on by Antony and Cleopatra, known to history if not to this play as "the Donations of Alexandria". Antony has publicly conferred on Cleopatra and her three sons various titles, "Absolute queen", "kings of kings", and various domains including Egypt, Cyprus, Parthia, Armenia, Syria, and Phoenicia. Cleopatra has appeared "In th'habiliments of the goddess Isis". Quite a performance.

We do not hear much about sons in this play. The one we see and hear most of is Sextus Pompeius, who speaks of himself as his father's avenger. He is the nearest thing to this play's Laertes or Fortinbras, and like them he seems to belong to an earlier era, still to be living in the world of *Julius Caesar*. Everyone else has moved on, even Mark Antony. As for these Egyptian sons, they are just pawns in the political game. Cleopatra does remember near the end to ask Caesar if her son can be allowed to reign in Egypt. (He will not.) But think how much Shakespeare could have made of these children, if he had wanted to.

What's striking about this whole scene is young Caesar's interest in the management of spectacle and command of "intelligence". This is most obvious when his sister arrives and he reels off the list of all "[T]he kings o'th'earth" assembling in preparation for war: "Bocchus, the King of Libya; Archilaus / Of Cappadocia..." and seven more names. It's the kind of speech that gets cut in modern productions, but it's a revealing one. Caesar is showing off to his sister (and his advisors). Look what I know! This is what it takes to run the modern world: not eating strange flesh on the Alps, or lurching around the battlefield with a big sword, but having good information, and knowing all the details.

So no wonder he is aghast when his sister arrives unannounced.

> *You come not*
> *Like Caesar's sister: the wife of Antony*
> *Should have an army for an usher...*
> *But you are come*
> *A market-maid to Rome, and have prevented*

It may be the most passionate speech he makes in the play, the negative equivalent to Enobarbus's great lyric description of Cleopatra's arrival at Cydnus. Now that's the way to make an entrance. What an opportunity poor Octavia has missed. Of course her brother is angry.

How is Cleopatra's theatre different from Caesar's?

Caesar knows the importance of theatre, and so does Cleopatra, but their conceptions of it are quite different. The biographer Lucy Hughes-Hallett writes, of the historical figures on which Shakespeare's are based:

> The art of public relations is a very ancient one. Cleopatra, Antony and Octavius all conducted themselves in public as actors in a drama of which the symbolic code was thoroughly familiar to themselves and to their audience.

The motto above the entrance door of Shakespeare's Globe was "*Totus mundus agit histrionem*", which translates roughly into "All

Opposite: Eric Porter as Enobarbus in Charlton Heston's 1972 film

the world's a stage". In this play we barely see the battle of Actium or the final encounters at Alexandria. The real battle is between Caesar and Cleopatra for who will run the biggest show on earth. "Cleopatra was as adroit as Octavius in shaping the public perception of her own actions," concludes Hughes-Hallett. Between the lines of the ancient accounts of her career one can watch a fantastic pageant being performed, a pageant which is simultaneously a sequence of real events and the symbolic and immensely exaggerated representation of them. Hardly surprising then

CLEOPATRA ON STAGE

There are Shakespearean roles, both major and minor, in which it is relatively easy to excel. Cleopatra is not one of them. There have of course been actresses who have been admired in the role – Isabella Glyn in the 1850s, Dorothy Green in the 1920s, Peggy Ashcroft in 1953, Janet Suzman in 1972, Helen Mirren in 1982 and again in 1998, Judi Dench in 1987 (to speak only of theatres in London and Stratford-upon Avon), amongst many others. One of the frequent complaints from English reviewers, was that no English actress could satisfy. They were accused of being too intelligent and insufficiently physical, sinuous or erotic. Victorian reviewers felt able to admire "the Asiatic undulations" of Isabella Glyn, but a century later that Cleopatra declines to star in the pageant of triumph and humiliation that Caesar is plotting for her, all the way back to Rome.

Cleopatra turns everything to theatre, with herself as the star turn, directing everything from centre stage, whereas Caesar prefers to stay out of the limelight and direct from the stalls or behind the scenes. Not that Cleopatra wants the stage entirely to herself; on the contrary, a double act is more fun, especially if her partner is an agreeable foil, not as quick on his feet as she is, of course – just as Romeo has trouble keeping up with Juliet,

---

Kenneth Tynan opined that "the great sluts of world drama... have always puzzled our girls; and an English Cleopatra is a contradiction in terms". Our girls were born to play Octavia.

But then most reviewers (and scholars and critics) owe their allegiance to Rome rather than to Egypt. So too have the historians and poets from antiquity who sought to tell "The Story According to Octavius", as Hughes-Hallett puts it: "In the imagination of the Romans she was a barbaric debauchee and a femme fatale who lured their generals off the path of duty." In his search for the lead for his 1934 movie, Cecil B. de Mille is supposed to have asked Claudette Colbert how she would like to be "the wickedest woman in history". The havoc Cleopatra wreaks must be a matter either of beauty or brains, but not, Jove forbid, both at once. As her recent biographer, Stacy Schiff, remarks: "It has always been preferable to attribute a woman's success to her beauty than to her brains,

and Orlando is always a beat behind Rosalind in *As You Like It*. And then there is her supporting cast, Charmian and Iras, and Mardian the eunuch. Antony speaks of her as a queen "whom everything becomes", and "becoming" is a key, rather elusive word and idea in the play (as Frank Kermode and others have pointed out). Egypt is a place where everything becomes something else, one might say, save that the point is more in the becoming itself than in the something else it turns into – as if Egyptians live by verbs, while Romans live

to reduce her to the sum of her sex life... Cleopatra unsettles more as sage than as seductress; it is less threatening to believe her fatally attractive than fatally intelligent." (*Cleopatra: A Life*, Virgin Books, 2010)

The looks are important, but this is not a matter of personal "beauty", of cheekbones and profiles and figure and ankles – or even the historically famous nose. (Pascal said that if her nose had been shorter the whole history of the world would have been different.) As Shakespeare well understood, the crux is always a matter of theatre and performance, where "looks" are determined by all the resources and accessories, the wigs, the make-up, the robes and the jewellery. And money: this was what in historical reality drew the Romans to Egypt – its fabulous wealth. Of course Cleopatra has to look stunning, however that's managed, at least when it's a question of "ostentation".

Must Cleopatra be "black"? Or racially "other"? (Other than what?) The historical reality is that like her Ptolemaic predecessors, she was a Macedonian Greek, and that her capital Alexandria was a Greek settlement, as its name suggests, one of the great

by nouns.

This would help to explain the sense of continual "bounty", of things abounding, brimming over, spilling and flooding, like the kingdoms out of Antony's pockets in Cleopatra's great dream of him. A land of super-abundance, of infinite wealth and opulence, where things never run out. What a dream indeed: a kind of Arcadia, a Land of Cockaigne, a fantasy of eternal provision, as if presided over by some great maternal principle, of endless natural nurture.

cities of the ancient world by comparison with which pre-imperial Rome would have seemed a pretty provincial, slightly squalid place. The Romans speak disparagingly of Cleopatra's "tawny front", and she refers to herself as "wrinkled deep in time". So she does not conform to the standards of female beauty dominant in Shakespeare's own time (as witness the Dark Lady of the Sonnets).

Like almost everything about her, Cleopatra is designed to contravene the expectations – the "measures" – governing the conduct of respectable women in the everyday world of the audience or reader. In Shakespeare's time there were of course such women: they were often called whores, and from the Restoration onwards they were often called actresses. You could always find them abroad, where "standards" were different (and lower). Byron claimed to find the Cleopatra he saw on stage in London an epitome of woman. Though he enjoyed trying to excite the Cleopatra in apparently respectable ladies, it was much easier to forget about respectability and just travel – East. And he did ∎

Antony's naturally generous instincts find themselves at home in Egypt, welcomed and enhanced – and funded – by an economics that the play itself never spells out. No wonder Cleopatra loves a man who knows how to "spend" (like so many others, this word has sexual connotations), how to match her own spending power. Here's a tiny example of the effect they have on one of the play's many "nobodies". Antony is running out of messengers at last. "An argument that he is plucked," notes Dolabella, when he had "superfluous kings for messengers, / Not many moons ago". He has had to send his schoolmaster to the victorious Caesar. This man is given – or takes – his moment of glory: "Such as I am, I come from Antony." He could have stopped there, but no, he is laden with Antony's bounty, with a verbal excess that Caesar is not quick enough to curtail. He goes on:

> *I was of late as petty to his ends*
> *As is the morn-dew on the myrtle leaf*
> *To his grand sea. (III.xii)*

Caesar curtly replies – through clenched teeth, one imagines, for poetry, at a time like this, is an offensive irrelevance: "Be't so. Declare thine office." But then this is what Egypt does to you, an Egypt run by Cleopatra, whether you're the Emperor Antony or his anonymous schoolmaster:

you start to go soft, you become a performer, and the poetry just pours out of you. Which is exactly what Caesar is afraid of.

Why does Shakespeare make so much of Enobarbus?

All the main characters in Shakespeare's play – and many of the minor ones – feature in his prime source, in North's Plutarch. Shakespeare's one really major addition is Enobarbus, who is developed out of a mere hint into one of the play's key figures. What need of Shakespeare's does he meet?

The short answer would be that in the move from narrative to drama he fills the vacancy left by Plutarch himself, the storyteller who comments and controls and passes judgment on the events and his characters. Now they have to speak for themselves. There are other ways of doing this, or some of it, as Shakespeare shows with the Chorus in *Henry V*, and other more transient figures exempt from the action, like Rumour at the start of *Henry IV Part Two* or Time in the middle of *The Winter's Tale*. But Enobarbus is fully embroiled in the world of the play, and his own life and death is a major part of its meaning and effect.

In some respects he answers to a role that we find elsewhere, the friend, comrade, confidant, counsellor – as Horatio is to Hamlet, or Banquo to Macbeth. Even the mention of these two cases however makes us realise what a varied, taxing and dangerous position this can be, so close to a leading male figure. Or think of *King Lear*: Enobarbus is, for Antony, a combination of Kent and the Fool – the voice of common sense, of everyday prudence and worldly wisdom, at once combative but loyal. Yet one of his other antecedents in this position, the rough, hardened veteran at the hero's right hand is – Iago.

Enobarbus offers a wonderfully rich view of what service meant in the world that Shakespeare knew, where everyone except the monarch was a servant of somebody else. (Now we only talk of "employees".) He is not animated by beliefs, or ideas, or ideals, but only by personal loyalty to his master, Mark Antony. It is through Enobarbus that we hear most vividly of the ambivalence that Antony rouses in his fellow Romans, and what he feels about Cleopatra. What a brilliant move to put the great description of Cleopatra's first encounter with Antony into the mouth of a man whose admiration for her, and for the effect she has on his master, is all the more genuine for being deeply reluctant. It is similar to that stroke of genius in putting into Caesar's mouth the story from Plutarch about Antony's famous powers of endurance. As for Cleopatra's allure and charisma, all the Romans are divided between resistance, repulsion and

SIX QUOTES TO REMEMBER

> Let Rome in Tiber melt, and the wide arch
> Of the ranged empire fall! Here is my space.
>
> (I.i)

> O, my oblivion is a very Antony,
> And I am all forgotten.
>
> (I.iii)

> This common body,
> Like to a vagabond flag upon the stream,
> Goes to and back, lackeying the varying tide
> To rot itself with motion.
>
> (I.iv)

> Finish, good lady, the bright day is done,
> And we are for the dark.
>
> (V.ii)

> For his bounty,
> There was no winter in't – an autumn 'twas
> That grew the more by reaping.
>
> (V.ii)

> she looks like sleep,
> As she would catch another Antony
> In her strong toil of grace.
>
> (V.ii)

susceptibility. Some, like Dolabella at the end, are more easily charmed than others. Enobarbus embodies both the resistance and the susceptibility. Cleopatra draws out of him a poetry such as we never hear from him anywhere else in the play, as if he were speaking her language rather than his own.

And then, for this man to desert them both, but especially his beloved master. "Mine honesty and I begin to square": it is the humiliation of Actium that determines him, something he cannot forgive. But then he discovers that he cannot forgive himself for his own betrayal – "I am alone the villain of the earth" – and he dies, extraordinarily, of shame. The 19th-century critic William Hazlitt may not be alone in finding this "the most affecting part of the play".

Most accounts of *Antony and Cleopatra* focus on the deaths of the two title characters, but it is important to the rhythm of the play's last phase that we see three deaths and ways of dying. They make up a rising sequence, of which Enobarbus's is the first. His is one of the most miserable deaths in Shakespeare. The dramatist makes it worse by refusing him the dignity of a true solitude, giving him instead an audience of anonymous Roman soldiers, to whom he means nothing. The language in which he faces his end has a dry agony to it – he thinks of his heart breaking into powder – that we should remember when we witness the two very different kinds of death still to come. Antony's has a messy, absurd kind of realism that taxes even Cleopatra's resources to turn it into a work of art. But she does, more or less, as only she can. Enobarbus gets no such assistance.

How do you earn "a place in the story"?

Antony and Cleopatra were legends in their own lifetime. Very different from Troilus and Cressida, whose fame came later, as indeed did Romeo and Juliet's. The play tells us that "fame" is a matter of stories, whether they are true or false. It is not nearly as common a word in Shakespeare as "honour"; there are only 85 occurrences of "fame" in the complete works as compared with 681 for "honour" (though this is partly explained by the latter's double existence as a noun and a verb). In this play we only hear four "fames" as compared with 20 "honours", including this resonant utterance, of Antony's before Actium – "If I lose mine honour, / I lose my self" – and this, from one of his soldiers, afterwards:

> *I never saw an action of such shame –*
> *Experience, manhood, honour, ne'er before*
> *Did violate so itself. (III.x)*

Although both honour and fame depend on what

*Kenneth Williams and Amanda Barrie as Julius Caesar
and Cleopatra in* Carry on Cleo, *1964*

TEN FACTS
ABOUT *ANTONY AND CLEOPATRA*

1.
To become Queen of Egypt Cleopatra needed
first to defeat her teenage brother Ptolemy, whom
she had married for dynastic reasons. After a
failed coup she was sent into exile. Luckily Julius
Caesar had come to Egypt to oversee the family
feud and Cleopatra managed to get the upper
hand by sneaking into Caesar's rooms wrapped in
a carpet and promptly becoming his mistress.

2.

The 1963 film *Cleopatra* is infamous for its sheer scale. It nearly bankrupted 20th Century Fox, the first cut was six hours long and Elizabeth Taylor, playing the eponymous heroine, had 65 costume changes.

3.

Octavian Caesar became Caesar Augustus; according to the Gospel of Luke he was the emperor whose decree led to Joseph taking his pregnant wife Mary to Bethlehem to be recorded for a census.

4.

Are you "cold-hearted", in your "salad days" or does your beauty "beggar all description"? All these phrases were coined in *Antony and Cleopatra*.

5.

John Dryden's 1677 play *All for Love or The World Well Lost* retold *Antony and Cleopatra* in 24 hours, without the geo-political scope and made the central characters more conventionally noble and virtuous. In the 18th century it was far more popular than Shakespeare's play.

6.

The Egyptian Asp was the symbol of royalty; Cleopatra believed it would deify her. However, a bite from an asp would have caused an unpleasant death, beginning with paralysis of the eyes.

7.

In *Antony and Cleopatra* we do not know what becomes of Cleopatra's twin children by Antony. In reality they were taken to Rome for a triumph and adopted by Mark Antony's long-suffering wife Octavia. Her daughter Cleopatra Selene became queen of the Roman province of Mauretania.

8.

In 1951, Vivien Leigh and Laurence Olivier performed two plays about Cleopatra, Shakespeare's *Antony and Cleopatra* and George Bernard Shaw's *Caesar and Cleopatra*, alternating the play each night. They took the plays to New York, where they performed a season at the Ziegfeld Theatre into 1952.

9.

Pliny the Elder wrote that Cleopatra won a wager with Mark Antony to produce the most expensive meal; after Antony had served her a sumptuous banquet she responded by dissolving one of her priceless pearls in a vial of vinegar and drinking it.

10.

Pascal wrote "Cleopatra's nose, had it been shorter, the whole face of the world would have been changed" to describe the influence her beauty had on history. In *Asterix and Cleopatra* she is drawn with a giant beak.

Anthony Hopkins as Antony in a 1987 production at the Olivier Theatre, London

other people think and say of you, honour depends more closely on your deeds and cleaves more solidly to your self than does the airier fame, which is carried to and fro on the wings of "report", another key word in this play, as elsewhere: "if report be square to her", "the world's report", "report the feature of Octavia", "she makes a very good report o'th'worm" – and Shakespeare's first and only use of the term "reporter".

"Report" is as functional a matter as "honour" is one of supreme value. "Honour" is worth risking and losing your life for, something you *win*. "Fame" hovers somewhere between, as the range of its uses in this play suggests. Antony replies simply to the news that Pompey is an absolute master by sea: "So is the fame"; Pompey says to Antony that "Your fine Egyptian cookery shall have / The fame"; Ventidius acknowledges the risk of acquiring "too high a fame", and Antony taunts Cleopatra with her sexual conquests including those "Unregistered in vulgar fame". Add to this an anonymous messenger's description of Menecrates and Menas as "famous pirates", and you would not conclude from its appearances in this play that "a fame", "the fame", or even just "fame" was something self-evidently desirable or valuable. Until the very last moments, that is, when the triumphant Caesar magnanimously

Opposite: Henry Wilcoxon as Mark Antony in the 1934 film Cleopatra

declares over Cleopatra's corpse that she shall be buried by her Antony: "No grave upon the earth shall clip in it / A pair so famous." Their fame, his glory. No mention of honour.

Fame depends on a name. But what *is* a name, and what's *in* a name? At the end of this play, Caesar is the most powerful person in the world, but he is not yet famous. For one thing, it's slightly confusing that everyone should address him and refer to him simply as "Caesar", when Roman history is already well provided for with a rather memorable Caesar, this man's "father". Throughout the latter half of *Julius Caesar* we heard about "Octavius" or "young Octavius"; now he has become abbreviated – apart from a single mention by Charmian – to the more arresting, and impressive, "Caesar". Yet it is striking how many critics refer to him as Octavius, or Octavius Caesar, or Octavian. Not without reason: in reality he did sport a confusing variety of names (something which the extravagant 1963 movie *Cleopatra*, directed by Joseph L. Mankiewicz, puts to good use). One of the ironies that Shakespeare's English history plays bring home is that individuals *lose* something of their identity when they make it all the way up the steep bloody stairs to the throne, and turn from being called "Gloucester" or "Bolingbroke" into "the King". The same is true of Caius Martius when he acquires the title of "Coriolanus". Whatever his name is, Octavius Caesar's fame lies beyond the end of this play when he will turn into the Emperor Augustus. It seems natural to call him, as everyone in the play does, "Caesar" – except when they speak of him as "boy", or "the universal landlord". Nobody *likes* him, except for his sister.

"Tell him," Antony charges a messenger returning to Caesar near the end of the play,

> *he wears the rose*
> *Of youth upon him, from which the world should*
> *note*
> *Some thing particular. (III.xiii)*

Why, with the proper intelligence network and administrative system, a *child* could run the Roman empire. This is why Antony keeps calling Caesar "boy", not just because of the wounding age gap, but because there's just nothing "particular" about his young rival. This may tell us as much about Antony as it does about Caesar, but it marks a massive difference of temperament between the two most powerful men in the play. Antony is famous for the things he has done; they have made him a superstar whose name commands instant, universal recognition. It is on everyone's lips, though it means different things to different people: "his name, that magical word of war," says his lieutenant Ventidius. "That magical word of love," Cleopatra might counter; so too might

Enobarbus, and Eros, and all the "sad captains" and servants Antony gathers around him as his end nears.

All Shakespeare's history plays, both English and Roman, address moments of massive turbulence in the worlds they represent. But there is a much stronger vertical axis in the English plays than in their Roman counterparts. To the English histories the concept of monarchy is essential, and along with it go a whole set of beliefs about the relations between masters and servants, nobles and commoners, and indeed husbands and wives. All these are largely though not wholly absent from "Rome". So too are beliefs in heaven up there and hell down there. In all kinds of ways the world is *flatter* in Rome than it is in "this sceptred isle". It is much more like our modern world in the West now than the worlds of *Hamlet, King Lear* and *Macbeth*. In a world as horizontal and multitudinous as this, the possibilities of making a name for yourself are as great as the dangers of dropping out of sight, into oblivion. What all these Romans want, or think that they want, is to "earn a place i'th'story", as Enobarbus puts it. How do you get into "the story"? Is "earning" your place really enough? Who or what decides whether you deserve your place or not? What does it cost and who pays for it? And what is "the story" anyway?

To take the last first: "the story" means the most

famous version, the one that has come out on top, the one that "everyone knows", like Shakespeare's version of *Romeo and Juliet*, for there are of course others, as there are of *Hamlet, Othello, King Lear* and *Macbeth*. The historical kings Macbeth and Richard III have been turning in their graves for centuries, despite the efforts of historians and other writers to redress the injuries committed by Shakespeare.

More than any other play of Shakespeare's this play teems with names: with those of characters we see and hear, often fleetingly, such as Varrius, Sillius, Camidius, Thidias, Diomedes, Gallus, Proculeius, Dolabella, Seleucus. Spare a thought

Mark Rylance as Cleopatra and Paul Shelley as Antony in an all-male production at The Globe in 1999

for Caesar's general, Towrus – and the actor playing him – who only gets to say the words "My lord?" There are characters who make an impression on us, and then disappear, murdered off-stage like Sextus Pompeius and Alexas, or simply ousted like Lepidus. There are characters we hear about but never get to see: major figures such as Antony's wife, Fulvia, and King Herod of Jewry; others in the distance such as Antony's brother Lucius, Labienus, Silvius, Caius Marcellus, Marcus Crassus, Pacorus, Orodes, Sossius, Photinus, Marcus Octavius, Marcus Justeus, Publicola and Celius.

Spare another thought for Hipparchus, Antony's "enfranchéd bondman", whom Antony blithely suggests Caesar may flog within an inch of his life in return for his treatment of Caesar's hapless envoy, Thidias. The scene of Thidias's whipping is one of the play's most shocking scenes. How easily the violence between the principal players spills over onto their underlings – for all the world as if Antony were doing to Thidias what he'd like to do to Cleopatra. But then, as Cleopatra remarks with breathtaking nonchalance, "Some innocents scape not the thunderbolt". There are ghostly names that appear in stage directions without ever appearing for certain on stage, such as Rannius, Lucillius, and Lamprius (though this may be the name of the soothsayer). Then there are all the nameless figures, the messengers, including Antony's schoolmaster, the soldiers, and the countryman with his basket of figs.

Particularly revealing are those whose names are uncertain, such as Ventidius, the conqueror of Parthia, who is three times in one scene referred to in the Folio as "Ventigius" – though of course editors "correct" this.

What about the Roman soldier who seizes the dying Antony's sword and takes it to Caesar? What is *his* name? When Antony calls for the "guard" a number of soldiers rush on. When he asks them to finish him off, they all rush away again.

ANTONY'S WARRIOR

Another mysterious figure is described as "Scarrus" or "Scarus". This is not a name ever voiced or heard or answered to in the theatre. It may be the name of the scarred veteran who appears to Antony just before the battle of Actium – he makes a point of his wounds – urging his commander to fight by land and not by sea, and greeting Antony's brush-off with the oath "By Hercules, I think I am i'th'right!" He has a brief but telling exchange with Antony's general by land, Camidius (or Canidius). He knows more than his superior does about Caesar's strategies and personnel. This fellow survives Actium and turns up again in Alexandria. Antony recognizes him, not least by the scars: "Would thou and those thy scars had

Except one, cooler than his fellows, who sees a big chance for himself. He will be the one to bring the momentous news to Caesar, and prove its truth with Antony's sword. Another Roman rushes on. We know what *his* name is because the nameless one addresses him as Diomed, and so does Antony.

Meanwhile the opportunist steals off, leaving Antony in his agony to the ministrations of the tenderer Diomed, and then to Cleopatra herself. The scene of Antony's death intervenes before this man's big moment arrives and he makes his entrance, with Antony's sword, to Caesar and

once prevailed / To make me fight at land". He has gone up in the world.

In fact this man is stepping into the vacancy just left by Enobarbus, the news of whose desertion overnight he breaks to Antony. He re-enters from the battle with Antony, who for a moment almost seems the junior partner: "O my brave emperor, this is fought indeed!" exclaims this soldier, who takes a curious interest in the new shape of an old scar – a "T" that's become an "H" – as if his body were something legible, a changing script. And this is the man whom Antony presents at the moment of triumph to his "great fairy", Cleopatra. "Behold this man", he says – if only Antony knew what his name was! It is some compensation that Antony calls him "my warrior" – the same words with which Othello hails Desdemona, "O my fair warrior", and Coriolanus's mother greets her son, "thou art my warrior".

But then this man sounds a match for Coriolanus. Antony declares that "He hath

his inner council. It is a great theatrical moment, or should be: the stranger with a lethal weapon. David Bevington points out that in Shakespeare's time it was treason to appear before the monarch with a drawn sword, and you can see why. It would be like walking into the Oval Office with a gun. It is this nobody's great moment, less than 15 minutes of fame, when he gets to name himself: "I am called Decretas." Is he? That's what the Folio tells us, here. In the previous scene it was "Dercetus". And in Plutarch it was Dercetaeus. Nobody seems to care enough to get it straight. One editor, M. R.

fought today, / As if a god, in hate of mankind, had / Destroyed in such a shape." Imagine yourself in this man's position. You would remember this great accolade, just as you would remember being allowed to kiss the same hand that Caesar's messenger got whipped for kissing. And you would remember the Egyptian queen calling you "friend" – she doesn't know your name either – and promising you "[a]n armour all of gold – it was a king's". Do you ever actually receive it? We never know, any more than we know

what happens to this man after the final catastrophic sea-battle. Antony yells at him – "Bid them all fly, be gone." And he goes, back into the anonymity from which for a few moments of glory he's emerged. Scholars and critics have laboured valiantly to establish his name, but nobody within the world of the play ever knows it.

In Shakespeare's company, he would re-appear as someone else, or rather the actor playing him would. For there's still a fair bit of the play to go and lots of small parts to be filled ∎

Ridley, goes so far as to say: "I do not know that it matters much what we call this unimportant character." Poor fellow. After all the trouble he goes to, the risk he runs to make a name for himself and get a good place with Caesar, and then centuries later, he's consigned to the trash-can. But for all we know, Caesar may have trashed him on the spot.

History gets written by the victors, it is said. They control "the story", or try to. But the victors do not always agree among themselves, the vanquished can never be relied on to stay silent, or to lack those who will speak on their behalf. And there are all kinds of stories to be told by those who were neither simply victors nor vanquished. In particular, Cleopatra's story is still being told and re-told, by Lucy Hughes-Hallett and Stacy Schiff and others, contesting and revising and exposing the excessive confidence of previous stories – and the agendas they seek to promote: from Augustus and his propaganda machine onwards.

What's special about the play's language?

In his early narrative poem, *The Rape of Lucrece*, Shakespeare treats readers to the dismal cliché that "men have marble, women waxen, minds". In this play everything in the

THREE 20TH-CENTURY VIEWS

Shakespear's Antony and Cleopatra *must needs be as intolerable to the true Puritan as it is vaguely distressing to the ordinary healthy citizen, because after giving a faithful picture of the soldier broken down by debauchery, & the typical wanton in whose arms such men perish, Shakespear finally strains all his huge command of rhetoric & stage pathos to give a theatrical sublimity to the wretched end of the business, & to persuade foolish spectators that the world was well lost by the twain... such maudlin tricks may impose on tea-house drunkards, not on me.*

GEORGE BERNARD SHAW, 1930

...consider the remarkable addition to the original text of North, the two plain words, ah, soldier. You cannot say that there is anything peculiarly poetic about these two words, and if you isolate the dramatic from the poetic you cannot say that there is anything peculiarly dramatic either... I could not myself put into words the difference I feel between the passage if these two words ah, soldier, were omitted and with them. But I know there is a difference, and that only Shakespeare could have made it.

T. S. ELIOT, ON CHARMIAN'S DYING WORDS, 1931

Romeo and Juliet want to escape from the family into a world that contains only two people. It could be a cottage, it could be anywhere. Antony and Cleopatra want to escape from the future, from death and old age. You cannot imagine Antony and Cleopatra retiring to a cottage.

W. H. AUDEN IN A LECTURE IN 1947

East is "soft", even time itself – "Now for the love of Love and her soft Hours". Everything in Rome is hard, rigid, solid, upstanding, like a sword or a pillar. To say that such an opposition plays into the terms of conventional gender distinctions would be an understatement, and this play tends to over-statement, at times near caricature. Hard things after all can soften, and vice versa. Hence the significance of all the rich language of melting, dissolving, dislimning, deflation, collapse, but also of things turning to ice, to stone, or to marble. "Go to now, your considerate stone," mutters Enobarbus. "I am marble constant," declares Cleopatra, with Roman firmness.

Egypt is everything that Rome is not, but the reverse is not quite the case. For the play tells the story of what happens to Romans in Egypt, not what happens to Egyptians in Rome. Shakespeare has no use for the time that the historical Cleopatra spent in Rome during her long liaison with Julius Caesar – she was there when he was murdered.* Shakespeare keeps her entirely aloof from Rome, and in this respect he supports her defiance of (Octavius) Caesar's efforts to annex her. Faced with the prospect of endless humiliation in Rome as Caesar's prize exhibit,

* Mankiewicz's 1963 two-part movie *Cleopatra* (starring Elizabeth Taylor, Richard Burton and Rex Harrison) stays closer to the historical record than Shakespeare; it covers the period of both *Julius Caesar* and *Antony and Cleopatra*.

Cleopatra takes steps to make a graceful, even triumphant exit. For this she employs every trick in the book – a kind of ultimate artist.

The critic Maynard Mack once identified a conflict between two primary kinds of language in Shakespearean tragedy. One of them is lofty, lyrical, romantic, seeking to rise high and range far; the other is everyday, down-to-earth, realistic, unillusioned, worldly. One pulls upwards, the other downwards. Othello and Iago are good representatives of the contrary forces. Clearly there is much in this play that answers to this rather stark opposition. It might correspond to the difference between Roman and Egyptian ways of speaking, between a plainness and curtness and restraint associated primarily with Rome, and an elaboration, ornateness and excess that's at home in Egypt. We have seen the two kinds of language colliding in that exchange between Antony's Schoolmaster and Caesar. We can hear the reverberant high rhetoric of Antony's "Let Rome in Tiber melt" rubbing against the coarse vulgarity of Enobarbus's "realism" – "your old smock brings forth a new petticoat".

One of the most memorable such moments occurs when, only minutes from her own death, Cleopatra launches into an impassioned elegy for her dead lover:

I dreamt there was an Emperor Antony... His

face was as the heavens... His legs bestrid the
ocean... His delights were dolphin-like... (V.ii)

It is the most magnificent vision of all Antony's best qualities transformed into cosmic powers and phenomena. We have seen for ourselves his human frailties. Now his bereaved lover sees something else, or wills herself into seeing it – and singing it, for these words ask to be sung or chanted. They belong to the world of grand opera, in which passion and vision stretch everything way beyond life-size. And yet all the time the man to whom she began by confiding this "dream", a Roman admirer, keeps trying to interrupt: "If it might please ye – ", "Most sovereign creature –", "Cleopatra –". That last is almost comically urgent and daringly personal. Finally, she turns to him: "Think you there was, or might be such a man / As this I dreamt of?" Completing her line of verse, Dolabella answers: "Gentle madam, no." This instantly sets her off again: "You lie up to the hearing of the gods!" He has told the truth, or one kind of truth, from which perspective hers is just an illusion, a fantasy, a "dream". This is exactly the position taken by Theseus in a famous speech near the end of *A Midsummer Night's Dream,* in which he scoffs that

Lovers and madmen have such seething brains,
Such shaping fantasies, that apprehend

More than cool reason ever comprehends.
The lunatic, the lover and the poet
Are of imagination all compact. (V.i)

This brilliantly manages to suggest that "cool reason" will never, after all, be *enough*. Cleopatra knows something beyond "comprehension", about the power of poetry to make things, to imagine what we *want*, beyond what just is – the world of may be and might be.

But Egypt does not have a monopoly of eloquence, nor does Rome conduct its affairs all in dry prose. These contrasts do not map neatly on to each other, and it is the swift and subtle overlapping between them that makes the play so constantly surprising. Lapping over is a feature of the play's own language, its propensity for images of o'erflowing, o'er-brimming, of flooding and drowning, for the elements of change and changeability – water, fire and air – for the presiding deity of the fleeting moon. "Over", or in its shortened form "o'er", is the play's most important preposition and prefix, as the verbs "o'er-count", "o'erpicture", "o'erpow'r", "o'ertake", "o'erthrow", and the striking noun "overplus" suggest.

The rhetorical figure that describes such excess is "hyperbole", identified by Rosalie Colie and others as crucial to this play, along with "paradox". The commitment to exaggeration and excess brings with it, inevitably, deflation and anticlimax. If this suggests something of the rhythm of sexual intercourse, then that too is entirely consonant with the play's own language. Nowhere is the pun or the quibble on "dying" (as death and as sexual climax) so central to a play's meaning. From Enobarbus's first bawdy jest about Cleopatra's "celerity in dying" onwards, the play implies such a close association between sex and death that by the end of it we find it hard to tell the difference between them. What are we watching when Cleopatra "dies" on stage (and Iras and Charmian)? Not for nothing, as Marjorie Garber has observed, does Samuel Johnson say that the quibble or wordplay was for Shakespeare "the fatal *Cleopatra* for which he lost the world, and was content to lose it". We can understand this the other way round, suggests Garber, that Cleopatra is herself the living (and dying) embodiment of a pun, or even the figurative power of language itself.

So we're listening here to something more than hyperbole, to a doubleness or duplicity or multiplicity in language, a slipperiness (like "the slippery people") by which words can always mean more than one thing. Hence all the sexual double entendres on such innocent little words as "broach", "go", "nothing", "moment", "cut", "case", "lap", "swell". An undercurrent of sexual meanings (to match the "overflow", if you like) that will finally materialize in the baskets of figs and snakes brought on stage by a rural fellow. As if this "clown" has been watching the play and awaiting his moment, somewhere behind the scenes or between the lines.

All this suggests that the language of the play supports or promotes an Egyptian rather than a Roman ethos, and it's hard to resist the conclusion that if the play shows Rome conquering the world, Egypt wins the war of words. Egypt will never become wholly "romanised", but Rome may become at least partly "egyptianised". Some Romans get this and others do not.

Take "likenesses", for example. Here is poor Lepidus being teased by Antony. When he asks: "What manner o' thing is your crocodile?" Antony replies:

> *It is shaped, sir, like itself, and it is as broad as it hath breadth. It is just so high as it is, and moves with it own organs. It lives by that which nourisheth it, and the elements once out of it, it transmigrates. (II.vii)*

Like the managerial and administrative language that now oppresses us, this succeeds in saying nothing at all about the crocodile. It refuses any risks, such as suggesting that a crocodile might be "like" something else. Antony is the kind of Roman most open to alternatives, and therefore readily at home in Egypt, where *everything* is like something else – so much so that a man might lose his sense of "distinction" between what is the real thing and the thing that it's "like". It's true that this puts a premium on finding new words – like new heaven and earth – to do justice to the uniqueness of this person, or event, or experience. Cleopatra does just that – though our ears are no longer attuned to it as Shakespeare's first hearers would have been – when she says over Antony's dead

THE LURE OF EGYPT

Egypt was infinitely less familiar to Shakespeare's first audiences than Rome. It still is. This is for the good reason represented by the play itself, Caesar's victory at the battle of Actium. If Antony and Cleopatra had won, the future of the Western world would have been very different. Its centre would have shifted from Rome to Alexandria; we might still be talking about an Empire and Emperors but the names would have been very different; we might have been as familiar with the gods and goddesses called Isis, Ra, Sekhmet, Ptah, Anubis and so on, as we are with Venus, Mars and Jove.

From the ancient Greek historian Herodotus onwards Egypt has always been the land of "marvels". For the Romans it was exotic, but not nearly as exotic as it was for Shakespeare and his contemporaries. Richard Madelaine makes the telling point that theatrical interest in the play has often coincided with the newsworthiness of Egypt in contemporary history: Napoleon's Egyptian campaign (1798-1801), the building of the Suez Canal

body: "[T]he odds is gone, and there is nothing left remarkable / Beneath the visiting moon." Michael Neill points out that "remarkable" would have been a remarkable word around the time of the play's writing, having only just entered the language. How like Cleopatra to "apprehend" a new word. Yet how like Shakespeare to ensure that the lines are still so memorable, even after the novelty of "remarkable" has faded – because of

(1859-69), Howard Carter's discovery of Tutankhamun's tomb (1922), the touring exhibition of The Treasures of Tutankhamun (1972-9).

At a deeper level, the play has engaged, especially over the last hundred years, with some complex anxieties and desires associated with colonial expansion and imperial enterprise – as perceived and felt, one must add, almost entirely from the point of view of the colonialising power. The play shows us virtually nothing about Egypt as a real political entity. It has much to tell us about Egypt's incredible wealth, luxury, and power, but it gives us no sense of how they have been achieved and held on to, nothing of the savage dynastic struggles out of which the historical Cleopatra emerged brilliantly triumphant, nothing of the politics of a country in which the Greek ruling and administrative elite were vastly outnumbered by native Egyptians. "[H]er competent and successful government of Egypt forms no part of her legend," says Lucy Hughes-Hallett. Nor, more curiously, do some of her more ruthless actions, such as the murder of her sister Arsinoe. This is, Hughes-Hallett suggests, because the legend is exclusively concerned with what Cleopatra meant to Rome and to Romans, to the history of the West ∎

the oddity, in those mysteriously simple, resonant words: "The odds is gone."

The play brims over with memorable and quotable phrases and passages. Its language works through contrasts both obvious and oblique, as for example in the comparison between two great scenes of festivity aboard ship. One is Enobarbus's unforgettable vision of Cleopatra's first meeting with Antony on the river Cydnus.

This is all the more wonderful for the relatively small adjustments Shakespeare makes to the prose passage in North's Plutarch. We should remember this off-stage vision created in our mind's eye when we see for ourselves the all-male junketing aboard Pompey's galley.* This lurching chaos makes for a profoundly ironic commentary on the vision of harmony, seduction and magical charm in Enobarbus's vision of Cleopatra. And vice versa.

On Pompey's galley as on Cleopatra's barge, there is music, there is wine, there is conviviality. But here, beneath and behind the festivity, we see the political realities, as understood by Menas, Enobarbus and the servants who introduce the scene, predicting Lepidus's doom: "To be called into a huge sphere, and not to be seen to move in't, are the holes where eyes should be, which pitifully disaster the cheeks." This is as extraordinary a

* Some productions, such as Peter Brook's in 1978-79 for the Royal Shakespeare Company, have made the most of the homo-social not to say homo-erotic "culture" of this scene.

sentence as any in the whole play, with its image of a dead or mutilated body, its suggestion of vacancy where you'd expect to find life and presence, its implicit prediction of the violence ahead when these shallow pretensions of concord between the top-dogs give way. Menas starts whispering into Pompey's ear. This is the moment when Pompey could become ruler of the world if he's ruthless enough. He is not. The boy's song captures the crazy absurdity of this moment – "Cup us till the world goes round" – when the fate of the world is in the hands of a group of drunken Romans, none of whom has the wits about him to realise what a career opportunity this is. Only a famous pirate called Menas. "Hoo! Says a; there's my cap." Enobarbus throws it in the air. Menas follows him off to get even more drunk. No Cleopatra-effect here.

What happens to Antony after Actium?

He falls apart, and so in a sense does the play. The structure of the play is in a curious way bound up with Antony's identity, and vice versa. Up until now it has moved between the two centres of power in Rome and Alexandria, but after the battle of Actium all the rest of the play takes place in the losers' domain. There has been an excursion to

Mount Misena, to deal with Pompey. There has been another to Syria that punctuates the collisions between Antony and Caesar. We reach what should be the supreme collision at Actium, but it turns out to be a terrible let-down. Why does Antony choose to fight there at sea rather than on land? Because, he says, Caesar "dares" him to it. How boyish, how stupid. And how shameful to toss away everything his long martial experience has taught him, and destroy his well-earned reputation for courage by abandoning his troops and fleeing with Cleopatra.

A pictorial and scenic theatre would give all these locations some credibility, as would the cinema. Yet in the Shakespearean theatre and most theatres now, behind all these different fictive locations we see a real material stage on which the true battles for dominion are fought out in shifting, overlapping, complex sequence – between Antony and Cleopatra; between Antony, Caesar and Pompey; between Antony and Caesar; between Caesar and Cleopatra. It is these contests that drive and determine the play's structure. First, the impetus towards conflict with Pompey (which dominates what is normally known as Act Two); the anti-climactic confrontation between the triumvirs and Pompey occurs about one third of the way through the whole play. Up until this point, the structure and sequence are reasonably clear. Antony is tied up with his rivals back in Italy. While the clock of political intrigue ticks steadily along, time seems to have stopped back in Egypt. But in the second major sequence the fragile concordat between Antony and Caesar breaks down, and the play hurtles towards the battle of Actium.

I say "hurtle" because something curious happens in these scenes at the centre of the play's action, scenes known in most modern editions as (III.iv), (III.v) and (III.vi). In the first of these we have the only husband-and-wife scene in the play, between Antony and Octavia. (We never see Antony and Cleopatra alone together.) Editors tell us it's set in Athens, but in the theatre we can't know this without some special effect. Nor do we need to know. It is peculiarly suspended in time and space, a scene that sooner or later Antony was bound to have with poor Octavia about her brother's impossible behaviour. Antony packs her off back to Rome. In about three minutes' playing time by the clock Octavia will arrive there to be greeted with miserable ingratitude by her brother. In the meantime Shakespeare creates another little scene suspended in time and space (III.v), in which Eros tells Enobarbus the latest news from Rome. Caesar has got rid of Lepidus, and we learn, with shocking casualness, that Pompey has been murdered. Suddenly we are in Rome (III.vi), listening to Caesar complain in turn about Antony, much as he did in his opening scene (I.iv). This time it's the massive spectacle that Antony and

Cleopatra have created in Alexandria, a ceremony in which Antony has made her an "[a]bsolute queen" and their sons, "the kings of kings". All of a sudden there's an uncontainable amount of news o'erflowing the measure. Here at the play's very centre, time suddenly seems to accelerate. Within a few minutes' playing time, and however long it has taken Octavia to travel from Athens (or wherever) to Rome, Antony has travelled to Alexandria and put on this massive show, *and* news of it has got back to Rome – all before Octavia arrives there. It's as if suddenly everything is speeding up and going out of control, and the structure of scenes enacts this.

After Actium, you would think it was all over, bar the shouting and weeping. And so it is, except that there is a great deal more shouting and weeping than we expect, plus two more battles, and the deaths, in sequence, of three leading characters. After Actium, we know Antony and Cleopatra to be doomed, if we did not before. What we cannot know in advance – and what always surprises both in reading and in performance – is quite what a long goodbye it will be.

Nothing in the play is more remarkable, and characteristic of it, than the speech in which Antony explores what he calls "the very heart of loss". Cleopatra has betrayed him for the last time, he believes, and as he prepares to end himself, he looks to the the clouds for an emblem of his own radical instability, his lack of true substance:

> *Sometime we see a cloud that's dragonish,*
> *A vapour sometime like a bear or lion,*
> *A towered citadel, a pendant rock...*
> *That which is now a horse, even with a thought*
> *The rack dislimns, and makes it indistinct*
> *As water is in water. (IV.xiv)*

So with himself: he cannot hold "this visible shape". Perhaps it is wrong to say that he falls apart; he has never been truly "together" and now he is melting away into nothingness. William Hazlitt thought this one of the finest pieces of poetry in Shakespeare, and made the good suggestion that we compare it with Cleopatra's later dream of her loved one:

> The splendour of the imagery, the semblance of reality, the lofty range of picturesque objects hanging over the world, their evanescent nature, the total uncertainty of what is left behind, are just like the mouldering schemes of human greatness. It is finer than Cleopatra's passionate lamentation over his fallen grandeur, because it is more dim, unstable, unsubstantial.

Is Cleopatra's death too beautiful?

Many of the play's most difficult questions are focused in Cleopatra's death. Almost everything Cleopatra does is "too" something. A. C. Bradley, however, touches on an important point when he suggests that there's something about her death that leaves us unmoved, or less moved than we wish to be, and than we are by other deaths in Shakespearean tragedy.

We need to see her death in perspective. It is the third in a sequence that begins with Enobarbus's, and follows on from Antony's – not as promptly as some of her admirers might wish, or indeed as Antony himself might wish, and as happens in other versions of the story which absolve her from the suspicion of angling for a deal with Caesar. Shakespeare could easily have chosen to make the lovers die together, or in close succession, as he had done with *Romeo and Juliet*. But he was intrigued by the lapse of time he found in Plutarch, and he decided to dwell on it, to "stretch" the play out further, to use one of its own images.

He was also intrigued by the description of Antony's death, the way he fails to kill himself cleanly and decisively, and then has to be hauled up to the Monument where Cleopatra has taken refuge with her handmaids. Both of these present

Katharine Hepburn as Cleopatra in a production
at the American Shakespeare Festival in 1960

real problems in their staging, particularly the latter, and much ink has been spilt both on how exactly Shakespeare imagined or required it to be done in the theatres for which he wrote and on how it has been effected in subsequent stagings. The crucial point is that Shakespeare has chosen to create this difficulty. Exactly *how* difficult is open to question, but there's a real problem, both in how you do it and in the audience response you aim to elicit. It is bound to look ungainly, cumbersome, undignified, slightly – perhaps even more than slightly – absurd. It is a challenge for director and designer and actors, but also, within the play's fiction, for Cleopatra herself. What can she make of *this* mess?

Here something that Bradley says of the play as a whole suggests an intimate parallel between Cleopatra and her author. Bradley remarks of the material Shakespeare found in his sources "how bulky it was, and in some respects, how undramatic". If that's the challenge that Shakespeare faced, then it's one that he sets in turn Cleopatra, when he gives her the task of literally raising a "bulky" body and laying it gracefully to rest. But this is what she's so good at, turning things into grace, making them "becoming", like hopping through the market-place. It is almost a game, as she finds the words to turn a brute bleeding body back into a beloved person whose spirit is passing away. Here's sport indeed, making it up as she goes along, as only a real artist can.

For her own death she has more time to prepare, and its difference from those of the two previous ones is all the more marked by its precision, the ritual care with which it's invested, the language in which it's performed:

> *Show me, my women, like a queen. Go fetch*
> *My best attires. I am again for Cydnus,*
> *To meet Mark Antony. (V.ii)*

As for the scene with the clown, this too seems designed to test Cleopatra's powers to remain in control, partly also to relax an audience all the more effectively to elevate us again in the scene that follows. Yet what do we make of the extraordinary moment at which Cleopatra says: "Dost thou not see my baby at my breast,/ That sucks the nurse asleep?" In the previous scene, she asked Dolabella a similar question about her dream vision of Antony: "Does thou not think...?" To which Dolabella replied: "Gentle madam, no." And one could say the same here in response to her question. But it would take a hard man – and there are no hard men present on stage to disturb her, but only the soft presences of Charmian and Iras – to say: "No, it's not a baby to whom you are giving the milk of life, but a snake whose bite is administering the poison of death." It does put the audience in a curiously suspended state, as if required to half-believe that there's no difference between a snake and a baby, milk and blood, life and death.

Sir Thomas North's 1579 translation of *Plutarch's Lives*:

1. THE LEGENDARY ANTONY

These two Consuls [Hirtius and Pansa] together
with Caesar, who also had an army, went against
Antonius that besieged the city of Modena, and
there overthrew him in battle: but both the
Consuls were slain there. Antonius flying upon
this overthrow, fell into great misery all at once:
but the chiefest want of all other, and that
pinched him most, was famine. Howbeit he was
of such a strong nature, that by patience he would
overcome any adversity, and the heavier fortune
lay upon him, the more constant showed he him
self. ... It was a wonderful example to the soldiers,
to see Antonius that was brought up with all
fineness and superfluity, so easily to drink puddle
water, and to eat wild fruits and roots: and
moreover it is reported, that even as they passed
the Alps, they did eat the barks of trees, and such
beasts, as never man taste their flesh before.

Shakespeare's *Antony and Cleopatra*:

CAESAR:

                                   Antony,
Leave thy lascivious wassails. When thou once
Was beaten from Modena, where thou slew'st
Hirtius and Pansa, consuls, at thy heel
Did Famine follow; whom thou fought'st against
– Though daintily brought up – with patience more
Than savages could suffer. Thou didst drink
The stale of horses, and the gilded puddle
Which beasts could cough at. Thy palate then did
                                   deign
The roughest berry on the rudest hedge.
Yea, like the stag when snow the pasture sheets,
The barks of trees thou browsed. On the Alps,
It is reported thou didst eat strange flesh,
Which some did die to look on. And all this –
It wounds thine honour that I speak it now –
Was borne so like a soldier that thy cheek
So much as lanked not. (I.iv)

2. THE LOVERS' MEETING ON THE RIVER CYDNUS

... she disdained to set forward otherwise, but to take her barge in the river of Cydnus, the poop whereof was of gold, the sails of purple, and the oars of silver, which kept stroke in rowing after the sound of the music of flutes, hautboys, citherns, viols, and such other instruments as they played upon in the barge. And now for the person of herself: she was laid under a pavilion of cloth-of-gold of tissue, apparelled and attired like the goddess Venus, commonly drawn in picture; and hard by her, on either hand of her, pretty fair boys apparelled as painters do set forth god Cupid, with little fans in their hands, with the which they fanned wind upon her.

---

3. ANTONY'S DEATH

When he had drunk, he earnestly prayed her and persuaded her that she would seek to save her life, if she could possible without reproach and dishonour; and that chiefly she should trust Proculeius above any man else about Caesar. And, as for himself, that she should not lament nor sorrow for the miserable change of his fortune at the end of his days; but rather that she should think him the more fortunate for the former triumphs and honours he had received, considering that while he lived he was the noblest and greatest prince of the world, and that now he was overcome not cowardly, but valiantly, a Roman by another Roman.

ENOBARBUS:

The barge she sat in, like a burnished throne,
Burned on the water; the poop was beaten gold;
Purple the sails, and so perfumèd that
The winds were lovesick with them; the oars were silver,
Which to the tune of flutes kept stroke, and made
The water which they beat to follow faster,
As amorous of their strokes. For her own person,
It beggared all description: she did lie
In her pavilion – cloth-of-gold of tissue –
O'er-picturing that Venus where we see
The fancy out-work nature; on each side her
Stood pretty, dimpled boys, like smiling Cupids,
With divers-coloured fans, whose wind did seem
To glow the delicate cheeks which they did cool,
And what they undid did. (II.ii)

ANTONY:

The miserable change now at my end
Lament nor sorrow at, but please your thoughts
In feeding them with those my former fortunes,
Wherein I lived the greatest prince o'th'world,
The noblest; and do now not basely die,
Not cowardly put off my helmet to
My countryman – a Roman, by a Roman
Valiantly vanquished. Now my spirit is going,
I can no more.

CLEOPATRA:

Noblest of men, woot dye?
Hast thou no care of me – shall I abide
In this dull world, which in thy absence is
No better than a sty? O, see, my women,
The crown o'th'earth doth melt. (IV.xv)

Does it still make sense to think of the play as a tragedy?

We use the term "tragedy" in more than one sense. One could simply say that the editors of the First Folio class it amongst the tragedies, and that settles the matter. But of course it does not, unless the only alternatives are "comedy" and "history", and even then there's a good case for thinking of this play as belonging to the group of "Roman history plays", along with *Julius Caesar* and *Coriolanus*. The boundary between "tragedy" and "history" was for Shakespeare a permeable one, as *Richard II* and *Richard III* attest; even *King Lear* can be thought of, according to one of its title pages, as a "History".

But these categories are absurdly inadequate for dealing with the "infinite variety" of Shakespearean drama, which enjoys playing with the expectations and conventions of genre – in much the same spirit as Cleopatra enjoys teasing, undermining and overwhelming Roman rigidities. To ask if this play is "really" a tragedy is already a rather Roman question. "Oh I like your Boston 'reallys'!" exclaims a sophisticated Parisian in Henry James's novel *The Ambassadors*, teasing the bewildered earnest American who keeps asking, of the novel's Cleopatra-figure: "Is she bad?" The imagery of melting forms and dissolving boundaries so central to the play also applies to its own shape.

Nevertheless the play does represent great historical events and the death of several main characters, not to mention a multitude of others offstage, and it is worth thinking hard about the spirit in which it does so. A. C. Bradley and others have worried intelligently about the difference of this play, and the other two mature Roman plays, from the four promoted by Bradley himself, and still generally accepted as – for all the differences between them – Shakespeare's greatest tragedies: *Hamlet, Othello, King Lear* and *Macbeth.* The word "greatest" is the problem. Bradley tries to do *Antony and Cleopatra* justice. He says that it does not strive for the same effects or achievements as the great four, and as for what it does achieve, that is magnificent. But for all his efforts to be fair, he is constantly measuring it against them, and finding it fail. Why? Because it does not stir in us what are, according to the time-honoured formula of Aristotle, the tragic emotions of pity and fear. We are just not made to care enough about the leading characters, Bradley suggests, or more to the point, not made to feel enough pain at their downfall and death. Indeed, we may even feel a kind of pain at our failure to feel the pain we were hoping or expecting to, the kind we *ought* to feel in tragedy.

The last two pages of Bradley's lecture explore these doubts and anxieties:

Why is it that, although we close the book [sic] in a triumph which is more than reconciliation, this is mingled, as we look back on the story, with a sadness so peculiar, almost the sadness of disenchantment? Is it that, when the glow has faded, Cleopatra's ecstasy comes to appear, I would not say factitious, but an effort strained and prodigious as well as glorious, not, like Othello's last speech, the final expression of character, of thoughts and emotions which have dominated a whole life? Perhaps this is so, but there is something more, something that sounds paradoxical: we are saddened by the fact that the catastrophe saddens us so little; it pains us that we should feel so much triumph and pleasure... we do not mourn, as we mourn for the love of Romeo or Othello, that a thing so bright and good should die. And the fact that we mourn so little saddens us.

Bradley has previously suggested that, for all the brilliant spectacle the play presents, a "painful sense of hollowness oppresses us. We know too well what must happen in a world so splendid, so false, and so petty."

John Bayley takes up this line of thought in an argument that distinguishes sharply between these Roman plays and what he calls the "tragedies of consciousness" in the great four. The leading characters in the Roman plays do not have the kind of inner depth we find in Hamlet, Othello, Lear and Macbeth. "In the tragedies of consciousness inner being grows and intensifies: in the Roman tragedies the external self stands up to the end, until it is struck down or strikes down itself." This doesn't sound true of Antony, whose "external self" collapses every time it "stands up", with a predictability that borders on comedy. Indeed this is the kind of predictability that Henri Bergson thought was the essence of comedy, when human beings behave with the mindlessness of animals or machines. Bayley himself writes well of Antony's "consciousness", that it is hurried helplessly from one moment to the next, in a way that answers rather surprisingly to the effect that writers like Virginia Woolf have helped us imagine as a "stream of consciousness". Antony's surrender at Actium is one response to the sense of fatality which dominates this pagan world, and which would once have been explained simply in those terms. Some individuals, like the Caesars, have a massive will-to-power, but none of these pagans has a soul.

But supposing that we relax or even abandon traditional assumptions about "the tragic emotions", and that we treat with scepticism the possibility of knowing what goes on inside a tragic character, no matter how garrulous or reticent he or she may be. Then we might recognise in *Antony and Cleopatra* a kind of tragedy less intimately focused in the fate of one or even two individuals. It would be a kind of tragedy in which pain is as much dispersed across the whole extent of the play as it is concentrated in a single climax. And it would be a kind of tragedy that invites us to question our own responses to this sequence of events, permitting us to identify ourselves with a vast range of characters, victors and victims and those caught or swallowed up in the middle. This would be a vision of tragedy particularly congenial to a modern perspective, in which we have learned to be more generally sceptical about

THE PLAY IN PERFORMANCE

In the theatre we are often puzzled to know who is who, where they are, when one scene ends and another begins. Everything is clearer in print, especially in modern editions. On the page editors can assist readers by providing a note on the venue. This practice began in the 18th century and continues, in some editions, to the present day, albeit often discreetly.

Much more obvious, and continuing, are the divisions of the text into Acts and Scenes, which provide readers (and actors and directors) with a handy way of knowing "where we are" in the play. Some printed texts from Shakespeare's own times have such act and

"great" individuals, about the power of choice in the face of unknowable and often unnameable forces at once outside and inside us, about the possibility of communicating our own deepest pains and staunching, let alone healing, those of others. The brute materials of tragedy may not change much over time, but the art of representing them has certainly done so, not least because the technologies for doing so, on stage, screen and page, have developed out of all recognition. We might conclude that in composing *Antony and Cleopatra* Shakespeare extended the art of tragedy in ways that have only achieved recognition in the

---

scene divisions but this play does not. Or to be exact, the Folio text announces "Actus primus, scaena prima" at the start – and never progresses beyond it. An innocent reader might think the whole play was a single enormous opening scene, without sequel, just hundreds of entrances and exits. (The Folio contains some important stage directions, as for example "Enter Ventidius, as it were in triumph, the dead body of Pacorus borne before him", and "Musicke of the Hoboyes [oboes] is under the Stage", and "They heave Antony aloft to Cleopatra.")

In performance the play can of course be divided up by changes of scenery (and lighting and music); in the Victorian theatre such visual machinery was very elaborate (and made for a long evening, had anything like the full text of the play been performed). The "spectacular" approach to *Antony and Cleopatra* reached a climax in the early 20th century with Herbert Beerbohm Tree's 1906

last hundred years, to the point where this play speaks as powerfully to us now as *Hamlet* did to the 19th century and *King Lear* to the 20th.

So much comes down to what we make of Cleopatra. Along with Hamlet and Falstaff, she is a figure whom Shakespeare endows with mythic proportions. And yet unlike them, she is a real figure from history, a legend in her own time, and ever after. If we interpret the play as her *triumph*, then we can understand it and see it thus, with Janet Adelman: "in its interpretative openness, its expansive playfulness, its imaginative abundance, it seems to me to lead directly to *The Winter's Tale*, where trust in female process similarly bursts

---

production at His Majesty's Theatre.

But one of the reasons for the play's increased popularity in performance since the 1920s has been the renewed enthusiasm for staging conventions closer to those of Shakespeare's own theatres, comparatively unimpeded by "scenery". They allow the audience to experience the action as a continuous flow such as we now associate with the movies. Indeed film has become a regular point of reference for a play which involves many rapid changes of scene and perspective, especially in the build-up to battle and its aftermath, a style for which the word "cinematic" has become convenient shorthand. Looking back to Dryden and the Restoration, we can see this as the kind of play that infuriated neo-classicists championing "the unities" of time and space.

However, there is more than usual point here to Shakespeare's exploitation of native and popular English conventions that

the boundaries of the tragic form". She is thinking of the figure of the mother in that play, Queen Hermione, and the children to whom she gives birth, through the force of "great creating nature". Nicholas Royle suggests something similar when he proposes that the play "seems to work through its tragic structure and come out somewhere on the other side, in a space of strange exhilaration, playfulness and joy". This is to give maximum value to the spirit in which Cleopatra arranges her own magical exit.

Perhaps. It would be a heroic achievement indeed to burst the boundaries of the tragic form and come out on the other side in a kind of

permit endless shifts in time and space. For these mirror the matter of the play itself: on the one hand, the Roman commitment to order, regularity and containment, and on the other, the Egyptian impulse to fluency, excess and unpredictability. Editors who label scenes and acts are engaging in a distinctly Roman activity, seeking to check, divide, and control the "Egyptian" flow of experience and phenomena. But for a theatre audience, performance tilts the balance towards a more Egyptian response to the running sequence they see and hear. It is more chancy, a more hit-and-miss experience; we see some things and miss others; we hear (and understand) some lines better than others. If only we could touch the pause button every now and then, to work out what someone has just said. Antony for example – it sounds like "our ills told us / Is as our earing" – but what does that mean? ■

paradise, the "new heaven, new earth" imagined by Antony at the play's start. It is tempting to identify with a force of nature like the Nile or the process of giving birth or endlessly renewable sexual passion. Antony and Cleopatra make their escape from living history through death, but their play does not permit us to do so. Nor does it put as much faith in "the law and process of great nature" as *The Winter's Tale* does, and other plays in which the hope of renewal and the prospect of futurity are invested in children – even in as black a play as *Macbeth*. However challenged and distended, in *Antony and Cleopatra* the boundaries of tragedy do seem to hold, however precariously, at a point just before they give way – or give birth – to something else, that would indeed be a new world and another play. That is what makes *this* play's particular greatness.

A SHORT CHRONOLOGY

83 BC January 14 Mark Antony born

69 BC Cleopatra born in Alexandria

41 BC-40 BC Antony spends the winter with Cleopatra in Alexandria

30 BC August 12 Cleopatra dies

1564 Shakespeare born in Stratford-upon-Avon

1579 Translation by Sir Thomas North of Plutarch's "Life of Mark Antony" from *Lives of the Noble Grecians and Romans Compared Together.*

1623 *Antony and Cleopatra* printed as part of the First Folio

1678 John Dryden's *All for Love, or The World Well Lost* produced and published

1813 Lord Byron goes to see a version of the play which he describes as "a salad of Shakespeare and Dryden".

1922 T. S. Eliot publishes *The Waste Land* in which he re-works *Antony and Cleopatra's* most famous speech, the description of Cleopatra's first meeting with Antony on the river Cydnus.

1929 Virginia Woolf publishes her essay "A Room of One's Own" in which she praises the genius of Shakespeare and *Antony and Cleopatra.*

1947 Katharine Cornell wins a Tony Award for her Broadway performance of Cleopatra opposite the Antony of Godfrey Tearle. It ran for 126 performances, the longest run of the play in Broadway history.

1963 *Cleopatra* film adaptation starring Elizabeth Taylor as Cleopatra and Richard Burton as Mark Antony released. Infamous for nearly bankrupting Twentieth Century Fox. The budget eventually totalled $44 million, making the movie at the time the most costly ever made.

The Meeting of Antony and Cleopatra, *41 B.C., Lawrence Alma-Tadema. The painting sold for $29.2 million in 2011*

BIBLIOGRAPHY

Adelman, Janet, *The Common Liar: An Essay on 'Antony and Cleopatra'*, Yale University Press, 1973. Also, 'Making Defect Perfection: Imagining Male Bounty in *Timon of Athens* and *Antony and Cleopatra'*, in *Suffocating Mothers: Fantasies of Maternal Origin in Shakespeare's Plays, Hamlet to The Tempest*, Routledge, 1992

Auden, W.H., *Lectures on Shakespeare*, Princeton, 2000

Barton, Anne, '"Nature's piece 'gainst fancy": the divided catastrophe in *Antony and Cleopatra*', in *Essays, Mainly Shakespearean*, Cambridge University Press, 1994

Bayley, John, *Shakespeare and Tragedy*, Routledge and Kegan Paul, 1981

Bevington, David, *The Complete Works of Shakespeare*, Longman, 2008

Bradley, A.C., "Shakespeare's *Antony and Cleopatra*", in *Oxford Lectures on Poetry*, Macmillan, 1909

Charnes, Linda, *Notorious Identity: Materializing the Subject in Shakespeare*, Harvard University Press, 1993

Garber, Marjorie, 'Fatal Cleopatra', in *Profiling Shakespeare*, Routledge, 2008

Gillies, John, Shakespeare and the Geography of Difference, Cambridge, 1994

Goddard, Harold, *The Meaning of Shakespeare*, University of Chicago Press, 1960

Hughes-Hallett, Lucy, *Cleopatra: Histories, Dreams and*

Distortions, Bloomsbury, 1990

Jameson, Anna, *Characteristics of Women: Moral, Poetical, and Historical*, Saunders and Otley, 1832

Kahn, Coppélia, *Roman Shakespeare: Warriors, Wounds, and Women*, Routledge, 1997

Kermode, Frank, *Shakespeare's Language*, Allen Lane, 2000

Madelaine, Richard, (ed.), *Antony and Cleopatra, Shakespeare in Production*, Cambridge University Press, 1998

Mirren, Helen, "Helen Mirren on Cleopatra", in Julian Curry, *Shakespeare on Stage: Thirteen Leading Actors on Thirteen Key Roles*, Nick Hern Books, 2010

Miola, Robert S., *Shakespeare's Rome*, Cambridge University Press, 1983

Mack, Maynard, *Antony and Cleopatra*, The Pelican Shakespeare, Penguin, 1995

Neill, Michael, *Introduction to Antony and Cleopatra*, Clarendon, 1994

Royle, Nicholas, 'Nod: *Antony and Cleopatra*', in *How to Read Shakespeare*, Granta Books, 2005

Schiff, Stacy, *Cleopatra: A Life*, Virgin Books, 2010

Woolf, Virginia, *A Room of Ones Own*, Oxford University Press, 1998 (first published 1929)

Williams, Gordon, *A Glossary of Shakespeare's Sexual Language*, Athlone Press, 1997

INDEX

A

Actium, battle of 89–93
Adelman, Janet 108
Aeneas 20
Ajax 20
Alcides 33
Alexandria, spectacle in 91
Antony
  Caesar, calling "boy" 71
  Caesar, relationship with 37–44
  children 42
  Cleopatra beguiling 26–30
  Cleopatra, sparring with 23
  consciousness 105
  death of 76–77, 100–101
  events after Actium 89–93
  fame 68–69
  first meeting with Cleopatra 60
  generous instincts 58
  Herculean, described as 30–36
  Julius Caesar's "son", as 40
  legend of 37–39, 63
  Octavia, marriage to 48–50
  Pompey, conflict with 90
  Roman view of 39
  sexual conquests, taunting Cleopatra with 68
Antony and Cleopatra
  critics 46–47, 79
  Dryden's version 4, 25

Julius Caesar, as
  sequel to 17
  language of 78–89
  likenesses in 85–86
  memorable quotes 61
  names and characters in 73–76
  performance, in 4, 106–109
  plot, summary of 10–14
  Romantic period, in 6
  sex and death, power and politics, about 17
  Shakespeare's lifetime, performance in 4
  subject matter of 14–19
  ten facts 64–65
  tragedy, as 102–110
Ashcroft, Peggy 54
Auden, W.H. 14, 79

B

Bayley, John 104
Bergson, Henri 105
Berlioz, Hector 47
Bevington, David 77
Bradley, A.C. 44, 94–96, 103–104
Brook, Peter 88
Burton, Richard 31
Byron, Lord 24–25, 57

C

Caesar (Octavius)
  anger at Octavia, reasons for 50–52
  family 42
  feelings for Octavia 45, 48–50
  intelligence, command of 51

name, use of 70–71
Octavia, sacrifice of
43–44
what Antony means to
37–44
Carter, Howard
Tutankhamun's tomb,
discovery of 87
Charnes, Linda
Notorious Identity:
Materializing the
Subject in
Shakespeare 6–7
Cinthio, Giraldi
Cleopatra 33
Cleopatra
Antony, sparring with
23
beautiful death of
94–97
beguiling Antony 26–30
boy, played by 22
burial 70
character of 19, 22–25
comparisons with 4–5
elegy for Antony 81–82
entourage 28
first meeting with
Antony 60
gypsy, strumpet and
whore, as 22
Herculean, description
of Antony as 30–36
legend, as 63
mythic proportions 108
race 56–57
Rome, kept aloof from
80
sexual conquests,
Antony taunting with
68
sons 42
stage, on 54–57
story, telling of 78, 80

supporting cast 56
tantrums 30
theatre of 52–59
Cleopatra (film) 65, 70, 80
Colbert, Claudette 55
Colie, Rosalind 83
Coriolanus 16–17

D
Daniel, Samuel
The Tragedy of
Cleopatra 34
de Mille, Cecil B. 55
Decretas/Dercetus/Dercetaeus
77
Dench, Judi 54
Dido 20
Dido and Aeneas 34–35
Dryden, John
All for Love, or The
World Well Lost 4, 25
46

E
Egypt
gods and goddesses 90
lure of 86–87
Romans in 80–81
Eliot, George
Daniel Deronda 5
Eliot, T.S. 35, 79
The Waste Land 14
Enobarbus 28
death of 62–63, 94
need met by 59–63
roles of 60
service, view of 60

F
"Fame", Shakespeare's use
of 63

G
Garber, Marjorie 39–40, 84

Garnier, Robert
  Marc Antoine 33
Gillies, John
  *Shakespeare and the
  Geography of
  Difference* 35
Globe, motto above 52
Glyn, Isabella 54
Goddard, Harold 44
Gorgon 20
Green, Dorothy 54
Greville, Fulke 41

H
Hazlitt, William 46
Hector 20
Henry IV Part One 37
Hepburn, Katharine 95
Hercules 20, 33–36
Hipparchus 74
Hughes-Hallett, Lucy 52,
  54–55, 78, 87
Hyperbole 83–84

I
Isis 21

J
James, Henry 5
Johnson, Dr Samuel 46, 84
Jove 21
Julius Caesar 16–17
Juno 21

K
Keats, John 5, 47

L
Leigh, Vivien 15
Lepidus 37
Lichas 21, 33

M
Mack, Maynard 81

Mars 21
Measure for Measure 38
Menas 68, 88
Menecrates 68
Mercury 21
A Midsummer Night's Dream
  82
Mirren, Helen 54

N
Name, fame depending on
  70
Narcissus 21
Neill, Michael 16, 87–88
Neptune 21
Nereides 21
Nessus 21, 32
North, Sir Thomas
  Plutarch's Lives 35,
  88, 98–101

O
Octavia
  Caesar's anger at,
    reasons for 50–52
  Caesar's feelings for
    45, 48–50
  sacrifice of 43–44
Olivier, Laurence 15

P
Phelps, Samuel 4
Phoebus 21
Plutarch
  *Lives of the Nobles
    Grecians and Romans*
    35

R
"The Rape of Lucrece" 78
Religion and politics
  40–41
Ridley, M.R. 77–78
Rome, Egyptians in 80–81

Royle, Nicholas 109
Ruskin, John 4
Rylance, Mark 73

S
Scarrus/Scarus 75–77
Schiff, Stacy
 Cleopatra: A Life
 55–56, 78
Sex and death,
 association between 84
Sextus Pompeius 50–51
Shakespeare, William
 English histories,
  concept of monarchy
  in 72
 famous versions of
  plays by 72–73
 history plays,
  turbulent moments in
  72
 infidels, awareness of
  40
 North's Plutarch,
  drawing on 88, 98–101
 Plutarch, use of 33
 report and reporter,
  use of terms 68
 Roman plays, stories of
  72–73
 Rome, plays set in
  16–17
Shaw, George Bernard 79
Shelley, Paul 73
Suzman, Janet 54

T
Taylor, Elizabeth 31
Theatre
 changing conceptions of
  6
Towrus 74
Tynan, Kenneth 55

Ventidius 68, 71, 75

Venus 21

W
Wilcoxon, Henry 69
A Winter's Tale 108
Women, liberation of 5
Woolf, Virginia
 A Room of One's Own 16

First published in 2012 by
Connell Guides
Spye Arch House
Spye Park
Lacock
Chippenham
Wiltshire SN15 2PR

10 9 8 7 6 5 4 3 2 1

Picture credits:
p.7 © Getty Images
p.15 © Getty Images
p.31 © CBS Photo Archive/ Getty Images
p.46 © Alamy
p.53 © R Lee/ Rex Features
p.64 © Alamy
p.67 Alastair Muir/ Rex Featuers
p.69 © Getty Images
p.73 © Corbis
p.95 © Getty Images
p.112 © Corbis

A CIP catalogue record for this book is available from the British Library.
ISBN 978-1-907776-14-4

Assistant Editor: Katie Sanderson
Typesetting: Katrina ffiske
Design © Nathan Burton
Printed in Great Britain by Butler Tanner & Dennis

www.connellguides.com